Eric Rodwell's
Bidding
Topics
2

Eric Rodwell's
Bidding Topics
2

Eric Rodwell

BARON BARCLAY
BRIDGE SUPPLY

Eric Rodwell's Bidding Topics
Copyright © Eric Rodwell 2019

Baron Barclay Bridge Supply
3600 Chamberlain Lane, Suite 206
Louisville. KY 40241
502-426-0410
www.baronbarclay.com

ISBN: 978-1-944201-29-6

Cover design by Jessica Sample
Text design and composition by John Reinhardt Book Design

This book is dedicated to my wonderful wife Donna and all of my Rodwell family.

Contents

Introduction

This book, carrying on the tradition of *Eric Rodwell's Bidding Topics Book 1*, contains 9 new bridge topics. As in the first book, each topic starts with the most basic aspects, then moves to intermediate concepts and at the end, something for experts. This way the material should be of interest to a wide range of players.

I would advise working on 1 topic at a time, digesting no more than what you think both you and partner can absorb and apply correctly. There are quizzes to help you check your understanding. When you feel ready you can always go back and delve deeper into the topic. Of course if you are just curious about the material you can read more casually.

Once again, N.I.B. has prepared hands to use with their excellent partnership bidding app called "Ubid". This app allows you to practice bidding with your partner on a wide range of material, including the conventions I describe in both of my *Topics* books, before actually using it at the table. uBid is available for download from your app store.

I wish to thank all who gave such positive feedback on the first *Topics* book, inspiring me to write this 2nd book. I hope you all enjoy it and get a lot of benefit from it.

Eric Rodwell

1

Fourth Suit Forcing

Introduction

Fourth Suit Forcing means a bid of the 4th suit, first of all. Example sequences:

1♦	1♠
2♣	2♥: 4th suit

1♠	2♥
3♣	3♦: 4th suit

Playing 'Fourth Suit Forcing' means that the 4th suit is not only forcing, but possibly artificial. Looking at another basic sequence to see what options responder has with various hand strengths:

1♦	1♥
1♠	?

If responder is weak, which normally means 6–10 High Card Points (HCP) (can respond with less than 6 HCP if you choose, and with 10 HCP can upgrade to an invitation; this type of hand evaluation is assumed in all our discussion), responder has these choices:

- Pass;
- 1NT (if available);
- 2 of an 'old' (i.e. previously bid) suit.

1♦	1♥
1♠	?

- Pass: normally at most 7 HCP. Would have three spades to know that we are in a playable fit
- 1NT: 6–10, natural, doesn't guarantee a club stopper but one would normally be held
- 2♦: 6–10, at least three and normally four or more diamonds
- 2♥: 6–10, normally at least six hearts. Might be five strong hearts
- 2♠: 6–10, four-card support. Some advocate 2♠ with some 'maximums' (9–10) and three good trumps

If opener rebids at the two-level, responder's choices are similar except that 1NT is not available. This would be the case if opener had rebid 2♣ or 2♦ in the above auction.

With invitational hands, responder's choices are 2NT or three of an old suit:

1♥	1♠
2♣	?

- 3♣, 3♥, or 3♠: all natural and invitational. Raises show a real fit (four or more trumps for a second suit)
- 2NT: invitational. Would almost always have a stopper in the unbid suit

Most of the available bids are taken up for weak and invitational hands. With game forcing (GF) hands, all you have left are bidding game directly, or bidding the 4th suit. It is for this reason that the 4th suit is played as not only forcing but forcing to game.

Fourth Suit Forcing is used for these types of GF hands:

1. A GF raise of one of opener's suits.
2. A GF hand with a five-card major, looking for a three-card fit.
3. A GF hand with six or more cards in responder's long suit.
4. A GF hand with no clear direction (i.e. no fit at the moment but bidding 3NT isn't attractive either).
5. Slam interest, which could include any of the above types.

When I say a 'GF raise of one of opener's suits', I mean one with some extra values. With a minimum GF it will suffice to simply bid game, i.e.

1♥	1♠	
2♣	4♥	enough to be worth bidding game but not strong slam interest

I would say generally that bidding game shows a good 12–14 support points*, and using 4th suit forcing first, then raising, would show at least 15 support points, i.e.

1♥	1♠	
2♣	2♦	'4th suit (game) forcing'
2NT	3♥	shows a forcing heart raise, 15+ support points

* Support points (after found fit): 1 for a doubleton, 3 for a singleton, 5 for a void when you have 4+ trumps. With Jx or Qx you don't count both the HCP and the doubleton. With only 3 trumps, the count is 1 for a doubleton, 2 for a singleton and 3 for a void.

Putting your hand type in a box

Before you take your second bid, as responder, it is wise to consider what 'box', so to speak, your hand fits in. For example, on this sequence:

1♦	1♥
1♠	?

If you are raising spades, is your hand, weak, invitational, game forcing, or worth a slam try? Once you put your hand in the appropriate 'box', you can use the corresponding sequence to show your hand type ('box').

Quiz

What hand type (box) do you fit in? What is your second bid in the sequence below? Do you have a plan for your next bid after that, if applicable?

1.

1♦	1♥
1♠	?

a. ♠ K J 7 6
♥ A K 7 6 5
♦ A 2
♣ J 3

b. ♠ Q 8 6 5
♥ A J 10 4 3
♦ 2
♣ Q 10 9

c. ♠ A 2
♥ K 9 7 6 5
♦ A Q J 3
♣ 9 2

d. ♠ J 8 3
♥ J 10 7 6
♦ A J 8 3
♣ Q 3

1a. Bid 2♣, FSF ('Fourth Suit Forcing'). You have 17 support points (not counting the Jack and the doubleton in clubs as

1 point each (likely duplication). Your next bid will be to raise spades at the minimum level, showing 15+ support points and establishing spades as trump.

1b. Bid 3♠, a limit raise (i.e. invitational).

1c. Bid 2♣, FSF. You have both a five-card major, and a forcing raise in diamonds. Your next bid will likely be to support diamonds.

1d. Bid 2♦. You have a 'weak raise' but will accept a try for game if opener bids again.

2.   1♦   1♠
                                     2♣   ?

     a. ♠ A Q 10 9 4 3   b. ♠ A K J 7 5 4 3
        ♥ A 10 3   ♥ A Q 3
        ♦ 2   ♦ J 2
        ♣ 10 8 7   ♣ 9

     c. ♠ A K 10 7 6   d. ♠ A K Q 3
        ♥ 9 8 7   ♥ 10 8 7
        ♦ A 2   ♦ J 8 3
        ♣ K J 6   ♣ A 10 7

2a. Bid 3♠, invitational. Your hand is 'invitational, 6+ card major'.

2b. Bid 2♥, FSF. Your hand is 'game forcing, 6+ card major'. If playing strong jump shifts, you might start with 2♠ over 1♦ but I'm assuming that isn't applicable for you.

    Your next bid will be in spades, showing 6+ spades (you might have only five if opener raises spades next).

2c. Bid 2♥, FSF. Your hand is 'game forcing, five-card major'. If opener supports spades you bid 3♠ to set trump, otherwise you hope opener can bid NT.

2d. Bid 2♥, FSF. Your hand is 'GF, no clear direction'. You are not sure what your next bid will be but you hope you can raise 2NT to 3NT.

The answers for the follow-up sequences are of course incomplete at this point but we'll get into more detail later in the chapter.

Which are the possible FSF sequences?

As you see there are eight possible FSF sequences:

1♣	1♦
1♥	1♠ or 2♠*
1♣	1♦
1♠	2♥
1♣	1♥
1♠	2♦
1♦	1♥
1♠	2♣
1♦	1♥
2♣	2♠
1♦	1♠
2♣	2♥
1♥	1♠
2♣	2♦
1♥	1♠
2♦	3♣

* Some play that a bid of 1♠ is natural and 2♠ is FSF, others play 1♠ is FSF. A matter for partnership agreement.

There are some questions we'd like answered about opener's rebid:

1. Does opener promise three-card support if he supports responder's suit over FSF?
2. Does opener promise a stopper in the 4th suit if he bids notrump?
3. What length and strength is opener showing when he rebids one of his suits?
4. Can opener have length in the 4th suit?

Hands with no good bid

Either player can hold such a hand. Responder:

<table>
<tr><td></td><td>1♦</td><td></td><td>1♥</td></tr>
<tr><td></td><td>1♠</td><td></td><td>?</td></tr>
</table>

1.	♠ K 3 2	2.	♠ A J 3
	♥ K Q 8 7 6		♥ A K 10 8 7
	♦ K 9 2		♦ 9 2
	♣ 7 6		♣ 10 5 4

With hand 1 responder has an invitational hand with the shape to bid 2NT, but with xx in the unbid suit, clubs, that is unappealing. With this 'flawed invitational hand', you have these choices:

a. Overbid and force to game using FSF.
b. Underbid and make a bid showing 6–10 HCP, hoping to hear opener bid again if you can make game.
c. Make a flawed invitational bid, such as 2NT with no stopper in the 4th suit, or raising without a known 8-card fit.

Hand 1 doesn't look that wonderful unless there is a heart fit, so I suggest downgrading to a 'weak' (6–10 HCP) bid, and the ones that appeal most are 2♦ or 2♠. 2♦ might be a little better; it gives opener more room to show three-card heart support if he has it.

Hand 2 looks chunky enough to risk forcing game by bidding 2♣ FSF. If you play 3NT you want to be dummy (looking at your clubs). Opener can have a hand with no good bid over FSF:

1♦	1♥
1♠	2♣

♠ A Q 9 4
♥ K 2
♦ K 10 8 7
♣ 7 5 4

Rebidding diamonds or spades would show extra length. Supporting hearts would show three, bidding notrump shows a club stopper, and bidding 3♣ would show three suits. So, you either have to 'lie' with one of the above bids, or have an agreement about a default bid, i.e. one that says "either I'm bidding Naturally, or I have no good bid". I call a 'default bid' a 'Punt'.

There are several possible approaches to this problem:

1. Make the bid indicated by your shape. In this case that would be to bid 2NT.
2. Support partner's suit with a doubleton, with the idea that partner gives you the chance to raise again to confirm a third trump.
3. Agree that the cheapest bid is possibly a 'Punt' (the hand with no good bid). In this case that would be a bid of 2♦.
4. Agree that the bid least likely to be needed as natural is used as the Punt. In this auction, you are unlikely to be 6-5 so you could use 2♠ for the Punt.

What do I suggest? I think it is more important to know what your agreement is than to play the absolute best possible treatment. Recall that there are eight different FSF auctions.

My suggestion is this: the least likely natural bid is used as the Punt. So, you would bid 2♠ with the above hand.

1♣ – 1♦   1♥ – 1♠ or 2♠

I believe that it is better to save space, that is to play that 1♠ and not 2♠ is the FSF in this auction. Using my 'least likely' rule, that means opener rebidding 2♥ with the Punt.

1♣	1♦
1♥	1♠: FSF

1NT: has something in spades. Might be 3-4-1-5 or 2-4-2-5, as well as more balanced if your partnership allows a 1♥ rebid with balanced hands*

2♣: 6+ clubs. You could agree that this bid can be made with five good clubs and some extra values as well

2♦: three-card support. If you are playing Walsh, then you promise an unbalanced hand so you would be 1-4-3-5 or have a spade void (most would open 1♦ with 1-4-4-4)

2♥: natural or the Punt (no good bid). If you play that the 1♥ rebid denies a balanced hand, then you would be 3-4-1-5 or 2-4-2-5 with nothing in spades

2♠: four spades. Must be 4-4-1-4 or 4-4-0-5, or can be 4-4-2-3 if a 1♥ rebid is allowed with this shape

2NT: 16–18, 3-4-1-5

3♣: 6+ strong clubs, 15+–18

3♦: 16–18, 1-4-3-5

3♥: 5-6, just under jump shift strength

3♠: 4-4-1-4, 17–19

If playing the Walsh style, opener rebids 1NT over 1♦ even with one or two 4-card majors. Also, I think opener can bid notrump with a half stopper in the 4th suit: Qx or Jxx.

You might not wish to have such rigid definition of the various bids but if you do, these are my suggestions.

Quiz

What would you rebid as opener over 1♠ FSF?

1♣	1♦
1♥	1♠: FSF

a.   ♠ A Q 9 3   b.   ♠ K 8 3
       ♥ J 10 8 7   ♥ A Q 9 4
       ♦ J   ♦ 10
       ♣ K Q J 3   ♣ Q J 9 5 4

c.   ♠ 6 5 4   d.   ♠ A J 9
       ♥ A K J 3   ♥ A K 10 3
       ♦ Q   ♦ 6
       ♣ Q 10 8 7 5   ♣ K Q 10 8 3

ANSWERS

a.   Bid 2♠. You have not denied four cards in the 4th suit, so a raise of FSF is natural, showing a four-card suit. The shapes you might have are constrained by your previous bids.

b.   1NT. This is preferable to 2♣, which should tend to show a sixth club.

c.   2♥. This is the 'Punt', a rebid of your 'should only be four cards' second suit.

d.   2NT. Shows shortness in diamonds, spade stoppers, and a good hand. It is worth using up bidding space to send a specific message about extras and hand type.

Responder's third bid

Responder in most cases will pick his third bid depending on what opener's second bid was. In other cases, responder has a planned continuation regardless (such as setting one of opener's suits as trump, or rebidding his own 6+ card suit).

Looking at our example auction:

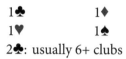

    1♣   1♦
    1♥   1♠
   2♣: usually 6+ clubs

2♦: 6+ diamonds
2♥: four-card fit, setting hearts, 15+ support points
2♠: this is a 'rebid' of the 4th suit, which I will discuss below
2NT: waiting for further description, natural
3♣: setting clubs as trump. Might not have been the original plan, but chosen now after the 2♣ bid
3♦, 3♥, 3♠, 3NT: we need to agree what these delayed jumps mean

Responder might have a strong hand with 6-5 (with five in the 4th suit). There are two ways responder can bid the 4th suit that might be treated as natural:

    1♣   1♦
    1♥   2♠

OR

    1♣   1♦
    1♥   1♠
    2♣   2♠

Since we don't need two sequences to send the same message, I recommend that with the 6-5 hand responder jump immediately in the 4th suit (sequence 1). This leaves sequence 2 as responder's own Punt. I would bid 2♠ on the above auction with this hand:

♠ J 7 6
♥ Q J 3
♦ A K J 9 3
♣ J 10

Responder's jump on the third round, if it means anything at all, should carry a specific message.

a. Jump rebidding his own suit shows a self-sufficient suit and slam interest. Any bid opener makes in another suit is a cuebid:

♠ A 10 3		♠ K 2
♥ A K 9 3	N	♥ J 8 2
♦ 2	W E	♦ A K Q J 9 8 7
♣ A 10 8 7 6	S	♣ J

1♣	1♦
1♥	1♠
1NT	3♦
4NT	5♣
5NT	6♦

The above is one possible auction. Opener doesn't worry about the stiff diamond after the 3♦ jump, and loves his AAAK. Opener could raise to 4♦ but responder will not be well placed missing three aces. Opener also might bid 3♥, which would be a cuebid.

b. Jumping to 3NT shows 15+ to 17 and is natural. This only
    applies if we haven't bid notrump yet:

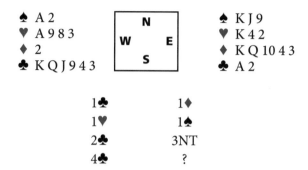

♠ A 2
♥ A 9 8 3
♦ 2
♣ K Q J 9 4 3

♠ K J 9
♥ K 4 2
♦ K Q 10 4 3
♣ A 2

1♣	1♦
1♥	1♠
2♣	3NT
4♣	?

Some agreement about ace-asking will be needed, but you
can rely on your normal agreements to solve such a problem.
Responder might also have raised to 3♣ at his third turn but 3NT
seemed more descriptive.

If you play the 3NT jump as showing extras, then you must bid
2NT and not 3NT if you just want to sign off. This has the disadvan-
tage of continuing the auction and possibly helping the opponents.

I can't think of a good and necessary meaning for a jump to 3♥
or 3♠ so I won't comment further on these bids.

Other FSF auctions

Time now to consider the other FSF auctions to see what I recommend for the 'Punt' if one is available.

1.	1♣	1♦
	1♠	2♥: FSF

2♠: either 5-6, or the Punt
2NT: natural, has something in hearts. I think you should be
    able to bid this with 4-3-1-5. 'Something' means at least a
    half stopper
3♣: 6+ clubs, or five strong clubs and extras

3♦: three-card support. Short hearts if playing Walsh
3♥: omit, as opener has denied holding four hearts
3♠: 5-6, just under jump shift values
3NT: 16–18, 4-3-1-5, heart stoppers

2.　　　　　　　　1♣　　　　　　1♥
　　　　　　　　　1♠　　　　　　2♦:　FSF

2♥: three-card fit. Can be 4-3-3-3 or 4-3-2-4 unless you agree
　　that you rebid 1NT with one or both shapes
2♠: 5-6 or Punt
2NT: has something in diamonds, might have stiff heart. Other
　　bids: like #1 above.

Quiz

What would you rebid as opener?

　　　　　　　　　　1♣　　　　　　1♥
　　　　　　　　　　1♠　　　　　　2♦:　FSF
　　　　　　　　　　?

1.　♠　K J 8 3　　　　2.　♠　K J 8 3
　　♥　8　　　　　　　　　♥　K 2
　　♦　8 6 5　　　　　　　♦　J 9 3
　　♣　A Q J 4 3　　　　　♣　A 10 8 6

3.　♠　A K J 3　　　　4.　♠　A J 10 4
　　♥　K J 2　　　　　　　♥　3
　　♦　6　　　　　　　　　♦　A 4 3
　　♣　K Q 10 8 7　　　　♣　K Q J 10 4

ANSWERS

1. Rebid 2♠, either 5-6 or the Punt.
2. Rebid 2NT. You have a half stopper in diamonds, the minimum for bidding NT.
3. 3♥. The jump raise shows diamond shortness with a strong hand.
4. 3♣. You have five strong clubs and extras, so 3♣ is the most descriptive bid.

3.	1♦	1♥
	1♠	2♣: FSF

2♦: 6+ diamonds, or five strong diamonds and extras
2♥: three-card support. Shapes depend on agreements
2♠: 5-6 or Punt
2NT: natural, something in clubs. Can have 4-1-5-3 or 4-1-4-4
3♣: I suggest that 3♣ shows either 14+ with 4-1-4-4, or 4-0-5-4 with 11+
3♦: 6+ strong diamonds, 15+–18
3♥: 15–17, 4-3-5-1
3♠: 5-6, just under jump shift strength
3NT: 16–18, 4-1-5-3, good club stoppers

4.	1♦	1♠
	2♣	2♥: FSF

2♠: three-card support OR the Punt
2NT: natural, something in hearts, not 5-5
3♣: 5-5+ in the minors
3♦: six diamonds, 14–18. It is commonly played that bidding diamonds-clubs-diamonds shows 6-4 with intermediate strength, hence this definition of 3♦. If you don't play this way, you could play 3♦ instead as showing the Punt

3♥: natural. You might agree that it shows either extras, or a spade void. In that case a 2NT rebid would not deny 1-4-4-4 and a minimum

3♠: 3-1-5-4, 15–17 or 18

3NT: 16–18, 1-3-5-4, good heart stoppers

Using 2♠ as possibly being a Punt is dangerous if you and partner aren't on the same page. If you don't feel comfortable with this agreement then you would want to either bid 2NT with 5-4, regardless of your heart holding (a reasonable agreement), or bid 3♣ with the Punt (I like this one less).

5.	1♦	1♥
	2♣	2♠: FSF

2NT: has something in spades

3♣, 3♦: as in #4 above

3♥: three-card fit. If you raise directly with this shape and 11–14, then you show an intermediate hand

3♠: Punt. Opener has denied four spades. At most xxx or Jx in spades with 5-4

3NT: 16–18, 3-1-5-4, good spade stoppers

6.	1♥	1♠
	2♣	2♦: FSF

2♥: 6-4 with extras, or the Punt

2♠: three-card support. Range depends on whether you raise directly with 3-5-1-4

2NT: natural, has something in diamonds

3♣: 5-5+

3♦: 0-5-4-4. Range depends on what you rebid with this shape. I recommend 2♣ unless very strong to save space

3♥: 6+ very good hearts, 6-4 or 6-5, just under jump shift strength

3♠: 15–17, three-card support, but not necessary if 2♠ shows this strength due to direct raise being made with a weaker hand

3NT: 16–18, as usual

7.	1♥	1♠
	2♦	3♣: FSF. This one is 'ugly' because it consumes so much bidding space

3♦: 5-5 or the Punt

3♥: 6-4+, 14–18

3♠: three-card fit, range depends on agreements

3NT: club stopper, I think it should show a singleton spade so that responder won't have to guess with a medium-quality six-card spade suit

Some more thoughts on the Punt

As you can see, having an agreement about what the Punt should be creates a lot of complications and stuff to remember. I discuss this in detail because in my observation most opponents seem to avoid bidding notrump with nothing in the 4th suit so it makes sense to clarify how to do so (in some cases more than one approach makes sense and I have noted these).

First of all, when partner 'possibly Punts', you should try to bid cheaply to give him a chance to clarify, which means rebidding the 'possible Punt' suit to show that it was indeed a natural bid.

```
    ♠ A Q 10 3              N          ♠ K 9 2
    ♥ K 2            W              E   ♥ A Q 10 8 3
    ♦ 5 3 2                          ♦ 9 4
    ♣ A J 8 3              S          ♣ K Q 2
```

1♣	1♥
1♠	2♦: FSF
2♠*	3♣
3♥	4♥

* 5-6, or the Punt

Responder doesn't want to bid 2NT so he supports clubs, counting on opener to rebid 3♠ if he has the 5-6 hand, with other bids showing the Punt. Once opener shows a doubleton heart, responder bids 4♥.

I should also note that the Punt, in one auction, consumes valuable bidding space. However, it is pretty specific so it is playable:

1♦	1♥
2♣	2♠

3♠: definitely the Punt, since opener denied 4 spades. If responder wants to rebid 3♣, 3♦, or 3♥ he is preempted from doing so, which would not be the case if opener rebid 2NT. So, you decide if you want to play that 3♠ is the Punt here. Or, agree that it shows 2-2-(54); with 3-1-(54) you must rebid 2NT even with xxx in spades, which is what I suggest. This way responder knows whether there is a 6-2 heart fit when opener bids 3♠.

Jumping in the fourth suit

I said that this jump in the 4th suit:

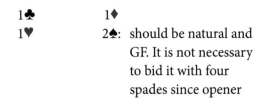

1♣	1♦
1♥	2♠: should be natural and GF. It is not necessary to bid it with four spades since opener

must 'raise' 1♠ to 2♠
if he has four spades,
thus this can be
reserved for 5-6 in
spades and diamonds

All other 4th suit jumps would need to be at least at the 3-level.

1♣	1♦
1♠	3♥: 5-6+, GF
1♣	1♥
1♠	3♦
1♦	1♥
1♠	3♣: discussed below
1♦	1♠
2♣	3♥: 5-5+, GF. Not 6-5 because hearts are lower-ranking
1♦	1♥
2♣	3♠: 5-6+, GF
1♥	1♠
2♣	3♦: discussed below
1♥	1♠
2♦	4♣: splinter, GF diamond raise

Some play that a jump in the 4th suit, to the three-level in a minor only, is weak with 6+ cards in the suit. You could have that agreement, or play them as 5-5+ and GF. Just clarify which way you play them with your partner.

Full deal examples and conclusion

Many of the late-auction issues depend on partnership agreements about slam bidding that are beyond the scope of this article, but I will give two full-deal examples to conclude our discussion.

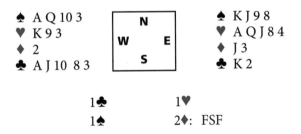

♠ K 6   ♠ 5 4
♥ A 2   ♥ K Q 10 9 3
♦ Q J 10 5 4   ♦ K 9 3 2
♣ K J 9 4   ♣ A 10

1♦	1♥
2♣	2♠: FSF
2NT	3♦
3♥	4♥

2NT shows at least a half stopper in spades. Responder shows a GF diamond raise (might be minimally GF since raises in a minor often want to wind up in 3NT or four of a major), and opener confirms a doubleton heart (preferably at least Jx). With a minimum GF, responder figures that 4♥ is probably safer than 3NT with a 2-2 ♠ fit and possibly no full stopper.

♠ A Q 10 3   ♠ K J 9 8
♥ K 9 3   ♥ A Q J 8 4
♦ 2   ♦ J 3
♣ A J 10 8 3   ♣ K 2

1♣	1♥
1♠	2♦: FSF

2♥	2♠: 15+, spade fit
3♣	3♥: cuebids
4NT	5♥: 2 keycards, no ♠Q
6♠	

Opener figures the combined values and distribution should make slam either a good contract, or cold. He likes the fact that responder couldn't cue bid 3♦, meaning his values were in the other three suits.

One final thought for now. In a two-over-one GF auction, 4th suit bids aren't needed to establish a GF, but I think they should be used as 'either natural or a Punt':

1♥	2♣
2♦	2♠: normally a Punt, i.e. something like

♠ J 8 7
♥ K 2
♦ Q J 3
♣ A Q 10 8 3

With four spades it would be normal to bid notrump now. If responder bids 2♠ and rebids 3♠ later, that would confirm 5-6+ in ♠ and ♣.

2
Minor suit transfers over partner's 1NT opening

Minor suit transfers

The original version of Jacoby transfers was just for the majors: 2♦ to show hearts and 2♥ to show spades. There were various less-than-satisfactory things done with a long minor: 3♣ or 3♦ responses 'to play', Stayman followed by 3 of a minor 'to play', or a 2♠ or 2NT response as a 'puppet' to the next step to allow responder to sign off in a minor.

At some point it was realized that if transfers are good for the majors, why not the minors also? It is possible to play '1 under' transfers, just as for major suit transfers:

OPENER	RESPONDER
1NT	2NT: shows clubs
	3♣: shows diamonds

Opener would have to accept the transfer regardless of what he had since responder might be very weak. This would open up a 2♠ response, which could be used to ask for minors ('minor suit Stayman').

Another variation would make a 2NT response natural and invitational:

OPENER	RESPONDER
1NT	2♠: shows clubs
	2NT: natural and
	invitational
	3♣: shows diamonds

It was eventually decided, by popular use, to play 2♠ shows clubs and 2NT shows diamonds. Each transfer is TWO steps under the bid suit. This means opener can bid the minor, or he can bid the 'in-between step':

OPENER	RESPONDER
1NT	2♠: shows clubs
3♣ *or* 2NT	

The distinction between the two bids opener can make is along the lines of how he likes the minor. It is possible for opener to measure the value in his hand in several ways:

1. Whether he would accept 3NT if responder has an invitational hand.
2. How well he likes his hand for slam if responder has that in mind.
3. Showing or denying fit for the minor. Many play that showing a positive hand requires at least Qxx in the minor.

You could use any of these parameters for opener's rebid. I am going with option 1 in this discussion. It is common practice for opener to bid responder's minor to say "I like it", and the in-between step to say "I don't like it":

OPENER	RESPONDER
1NT	2♠

3♣: "I like clubs"
2NT: "I don't like clubs"

If you prefer it the other way that is OK. There are two reasons to do it the suggested way however:

1. If responder is planning to play it in 3♣ regardless, then only one opponent gets to know this (after responder passes 3♣). This makes competing against 3♣ a little more difficult for the opponents.
2. Opener has bid the minor on the hands that like it, right-siding a possible contract in the minor right away.

So, try your rebid using my suggested rule: *bidding responder's minor shows the better hand for 3NT.*

OPENER	RESPONDER
1NT	2♠
?	

OPENER 1	OPENER 2	OPENER 3	OPENER 4
♠ A 10 8 3	♠ Q 3 2	♠ A Q 9 3	♠ A K 8 7
♥ A 9 3	♥ K Q J 3	♥ A Q 8	♥ A J 9 8
♦ A 8 7	♦ K Q 3	♦ K J 10 3	♦ K 3
♣ K 10 8	♣ K J 3	♣ 7 6	♣ Q 10 8

Opener 1 has a minimum, which is normally a rejection, but has a perfect hand for notrump if responder has 6 clubs to the AQ and nothing else, so he should bid 3♣, responder's minor, to accept. Responder can pass 3♣ if he has a weaker hand.

Opener 2 has a maximum which is normally an acceptance, but this hand is so poor for 3NT that I prefer a 2NT bid. Imagine again responder with 6 clubs to the AQ and nothing else and 3NT is very poor.

Opener 3 has 16 HCP and excellent stoppers. The problem is having the worst possible club holding, xx, so bid 2NT to reject a possible game try. With the ♦3 made into the ♣3, I would accept by bidding 3♣.

Opener 4 has the best of everything with a maximum, suitable fit, and good stoppers. Still, if responder has 6 clubs to the J and nothing else 3♣ is the spot so just bid 3♣.

Responder's continuations

If responder is weak, he will play 3 of the minor. If opener bid it, then responder passes. If opener bid the in-between step to show less 3NT interest, responder bids 3 of the minor and opener must pass.

OPENER	RESPONDER
♠ A K Q	♠ J 9 3
♥ 9 7 6	♥ J 8
♦ J 2	♦ K 9 8 7 6 5 4
♣ K Q 8 4 3	♣ 2
1NT	2NT
3♣	3♦

2NT showed long diamonds and 3♣, the in-between step, showed a weaker hand for 3NT. 3♦ is a sign-off. 3♦ might well go down but it is a better contract than 1NT.

If responder has an invitational hand, he can judge from opener's reply whether to stay in 3 of the minor or try 3NT.

Assuming opener has accepted a 3NT try bidding 3 of the minor, responder should try 3NT with AQxxxx or better in his minor, with KQxxxx and nothing else 3NT is aggressive but might work. Responder can also bid 3NT with a weaker suit and some side values, such as KJxxxx in the minor and a side king.

With these same holdings, if opener rejects the game try by bidding the in-between step, responder bids 3 of his minor to sign off.

OPENER 1	RESPONDER
♠ 10 7 6	♠ 9 3
♥ A K Q J	♥ 10 7 6
♦ 9 2	♦ A Q 7 6 5 4
♣ A Q 10 3	♣ 9 2
1NT	2NT
3♣	3♦
Pass	

OPENER 2	RESPONDER (SAME)
♠ A 10 4	♠ 9 3
♥ A J 8	♥ 10 7 6
♦ K 9 8	♦ A Q 7 6 5 4
♣ A 8 6 5	♣ 9 2
1NT	2NT
3♦	3NT
Pass	

This is not an exact science, for example, if opener had KQ65 of clubs instead of the A865 a spade lead might defeat 3NT since there are then only 8 top tricks. But, maybe spades are 4-4 and 3NT will still make. Or perhaps you will get a more favorable heart or club lead.

What about playing 5 of the minor instead of 3NT? If responder is balanced, 6322 or 7222, it is unlikely that 5 of the minor is better than 3NT, and if it is, how would we figure it out? However, it is a totally different story if responder is short in a suit, now we might have say a singleton facing three small. Not only are we off the whole suit for 3NT, but the rest of our high cards are working overtime to make a high-level minor suit contract playable.

Let's look at such a layout:

OPENER	RESPONDER
♠ 8 7 6	♠ 2
♥ A K 8 3	♥ Q 9 2
♦ K 9 3	♦ A Q J 7 6 5
♣ A Q 9	♣ J 10 3

3NT is off at least 5 spade tricks if they lead one which most of the time they would. In diamonds, you are laydown for 11 tricks and if the club finesse works you can make a slam.

The way most solve this problem is to have the following agreement: *transferring to a minor then following with a new suit shows SHORTNESS in that suit, and at least a game forcing hand.*

On the above hand, responder would continue with 3♠ to show shortness in spades and a game forcing hand. The entire auction might be:

OPENER	RESPONDER
1NT	2NT
3♦	3♠: shortness in spades, game force
4♣	5♦

Opener bids 4♣, a control bid, to show interest in a high diamond contract, and that he can't play 3NT. Responder has a very minimum hand for his previous bidding so he attempts to sign off in 5♦. No reason to be greedy and bid slam on every hand where it might have a play, better to take a more certain game bonus. Some might just jump to 3NT and go down off the top in that contract.

Some might wish to play that transferring to a minor then bidding a new suit is natural, showing 6 in the minor and a 4-card major. This is OK as far as it goes, but it means that the 'minor + shortness' hand we just looked at can't be bid properly. Most would say that with a 4-card major and a longer minor, game forcing values, you should bid Stayman then follow with your minor at the 3-level. This is game forcing and invites a raise with a suitable hand.

OPENER	RESPONDER
♠ A 2	♠ K J 10 8
♥ A J 9 3	♥ K 2
♦ K J 4 3	♦ A Q 9 8 7 6
♣ Q 8 3	♣ 4

This is another hand where 6♦ is virtually laydown, and 3NT might be down off the top on a club lead. A club lead would be more likely than normal if you bid Stayman and over 2♥, bid 3NT marking you with 4 spades. This is one possible way to bid these hands:

OPENER	RESPONDER
1NT	2♣
2♥	3♦
4♦	4NT
5♣	6♦

The 3♦ bid is game forcing with 5+ diamonds. Responder promises a major also, and when opener bids hearts, responder's major must be spades (he did not raise hearts). Opener's hand is ideal for a diamond contract so he raises to 4♦. There might be a bit to the play but responder has enough to bid Blackwood into slam. If you play different keycard asking methods, adjust the sequence accordingly.

In conclusion, transferring to a minor then bidding a new suit is GF, showing shortness with a one-suited hand, as we just discussed.

Handling a weak hand with 5-5 in the minors

Some like to play that a 3♣ response to 1NT shows a weak hand with 5-5 in the minors. Most have found this a waste of a bid for a rare hand, and prefer to use a 3♣ response for something else. Personally I recommend 'Puppet Stayman', a bid to ask opener about 5-card majors but that is the subject of another topic.

In any event, with a weak hand with 5-5 in the minors, responder can bid 2NT transfer to diamonds and pass opener's response. If he bids 3♣ to say he doesn't want to play 3NT there is a reasonable chance that he has clubs at least as good as diamonds. This is not assured of course since opener bids 3♣ to reject an invitation to 3NT when responder has diamonds.

Those who are concerned about this last point might require a 3♦ response when opener has better diamonds, regardless of his interest in 3NT opposite a long diamond suit. Every convention has a cost. In any event, here is how it might work in normal cases:

OPENER	RESPONDER
♠ A J 7 5	♠ 2
♥ A 10 4 3	♥ 8 2
♦ A K 9	♦ J 10 8 7 6
♣ 10 3	♣ Q J 8 4 2
1NT	2NT
3♦	Pass

If opener , with the minors reversed, he has a poor diamond holding for 3NT and would bid 3♣, and responder would pass.

Using 2♠ as either a range ask or a club suit

Those who use 2NT as a diamond transfer lose the natural invitational raise to 2NT. It is then commonly played that with such a hand responder must bid 2♣, then bid 2NT.

That raises complications in an auction like this:

OPENER	RESPONDER
1NT	2♣
2♥	2NT

Suppose opener has 4-4 in the majors – what does he do now? There are various ways of dealing with this problem but all cost something. Another problem:

OPENER	RESPONDER
1NT	2♣
2♠	2NT

Now responder has told the opponents that opener has 4 spades, and if he should have an invitational hand with no 4-card major, responder doesn't care if opener has 4 spades so this is only helpful to the opponents.

The solution, again at a cost, is to use a 2♠ response to ask if opener has a minimum or maximum hand, rather than focusing on how he likes his hand opposite a long club suit:

OPENER	RESPONDER
1NT	2♠: 'clubs or range ask'
2NT: minimum	
3♣: maximum	

This means that a 2♣ response promises a major. This actually gives the opponents more information if opener bids a major and responder doesn't raise:

OPENER	RESPONDER
1NT	2♣
2♥	2NT: shows 4 spades

This does make opener's bidding easy if he is 4-4 in the majors however. And, it allows responder to bid 2♣ Stayman and follow with a 2♠ bid:

OPENER	RESPONDER
1NT	2♣
2♥	2♠: ?

Playing the method where 2♣ does NOT promise a major, responder's 2♠ bid in the above auction is normally played as showing 4 spades and a raise to 2NT. Using 2♠ as 'clubs or range ask', this is not necessary – bidding 2♣ then 2NT shows 4 spades and an invitational hand.

Thus, many use the 2♠ bid in the above auction to show FIVE spades and a mild invitational hand, something like this:

> ♠ A J 10 8 3
> ♥ 2
> ♦ Q 10 7 6
> ♣ 10 8 7

This is the sort of hand that game will probably be a good contract if opener has a maximum with 3 spades, but otherwise you want to stop in 2♠. Of course over your Stayman 2♣ bid if you hear opener bid spades to show 4, you will like it enough to bid game.

More on 2♠ 'clubs or range ask'

Fortunately, there isn't much more to it. If responder has a raise to 2NT, he either passes when opener bids 2NT to show a minimum, or bids 3NT if opener bids 3♣ to show a maximum:

OPENER 1	RESPONDER
♠ A 8 7	♠ J 6 5
♥ K Q 9 3	♥ J 2
♦ A 8 3	♦ K 9 4 2
♣ Q 7 6	♣ A 5 4 3
1NT	2♠
2NT	Pass

2NT shows a minimum hand, not saying anything about clubs. Responder passes, wishing he had passed 1NT. At least he has not tipped an opening leader not to lead a heart from say A10xx by bidding 2♣ Stayman.

OPENER 2	RESPONDER (SAME)
♠ A 10 8 7	♠ J 6 5
♥ K 10 7	♥ J 2
♦ A Q 8 7	♦ K 9 4 2
♣ K J	♣ A 5 4 3
1NT	2♠
3♣	3NT

Opener's 3♣ bid shows a maximum and responder then bids 3NT to sign off.

Any other continuations responder makes having bid 2♠ over 1NT show long clubs, in accordance with our prior discussion.

OPENER	RESPONDER
♠ K J 8	♠ Q 10 3
♥ J 8 7	♥ K 9 3
♦ A Q 9 4	♦ 2
♣ K J 3	♣ A Q 9 7 6 5

1NT	2♣
2NT	3♦
3NT	

Opener's 2NT shows a minimum, and responder's 3♦ shows a game forcing one-suiter with clubs plus short diamonds. Opener has an easy 3NT bid.

Backing into a major suit game

Occasionally when responder has shortness in a side suit, opener will want to suggest playing in a major (not the short suit). For one thing, opener might have a 5-card major if he is 5332 (I do recommend opening 1NT with this but this is a matter of agreement). Another possibility is a strong 4-card suit on a hand that might play well in a 4-3 fit:

OPENER	RESPONDER
♠ A K Q 8	♠ J 10 6
♥ Q 6 3	♥ 2
♦ K 9 4	♦ Q J 2
♣ J 8 3	♣ A Q 9 6 5 2

1NT	2♣
2NT	3♥
3♠	4♠

Opener bids 3♠, seeking a raise with 3-card support (responder might have a 7th club, say 2-1-3-7, or maybe 4-6 in the minors so it is not assured that he has 3 spades). 5♣ is a reasonable contract also but only 4♠ has a chance if you have to lose a club trick.

Opponents double a 2♠ or 2NT response

The easy thing would be to ignore the double and bid what you would have bid had they passed. There are two new choices, pass and redouble, that you might wish to find meaning for.

I suggest that opener's redouble be for penalty, as it would be in this sequence:

OPENER   **RESPONDER**
1NT   (Pass)   2♣   (Double)
Redouble: penalty

In the above auction, responder does not have to pass if he doesn't think he can make 2♣ redoubled opposite a good 5-card club suit. This auction should be similar:

OPENER   **RESPONDER**
1NT   (Pass)   2♠   (Double)
Redouble: penalty

I would redouble 2♠ with this hand:

♠ A Q 9 8 3
♥ A 2
♦ K J 3
♣ Q 8 3

If responder has a raise to 2NT and a couple of spades, he should make 2♠ redoubled, knowing the spades are in front of your hand. If responder has short spades, or a weak hand with clubs, he can bid 'system on': 3♣ is a sign-off, 2NT shows a raise to 2NT, higher bids show shortness with a club suit and a game force.

If you lack a stopper in spades, you can PASS. If responder lacks a spade stopper also you might avoid a 3NT contract that has no play on a spade lead:

OPENER	RESPONDER
♠ 8 6 5	♠ 4 2
♥ A K Q 8	♥ 9 3
♦ Q J 3	♦ K 10 8 7
♣ A J 3	♣ K Q 10 7 6

OPENER		RESPONDER	
1NT	(Pass)	2♠	(Double)
Pass	(Pass)	3♣	

Originally, responder planned to treat his hand as a raise to 2NT and when you bid 3♣ to show a maximum, 3NT would be reached. When 2♠ gets doubled, responder changes his mind when you pass to show no spade stopper and retreats to 3♣.

This brings to mind a question: what if responder has long diamonds in the above auction? Would it not be better to treat a retreat to 3♦ as a sign-off rather than a game forcing with long clubs and short diamonds?

I think the answer to this is yes, but definitely not unless this has been carefully discussed. To see why this is useful, reverse responder's minor suits in the above deal.

What should it mean if responder balances with a redouble?

OPENER		RESPONDER	
1NT	(Pass)	2♠	(Double)
Pass	(Pass)	Redouble	

Opener has denied a spade stopper and responder has denied spades so a penalty in 2♠ redoubled is not likely. I suggest this show a partial spade stopper and a raise to 2NT. Opener can sign off in 2NT or 3NT, or bail to 3 of a minor:

OPENER		RESPONDER	
♠ J 3 2		♠ Q 4	
♥ A 8 7		♥ K 9 2	
♦ A K 10 8 7		♦ Q 9 3	
♣ A 3		♣ Q 10 9 5 4	
1NT	(Pass)	2♠	(Double)
Pass	(Pass)	Redouble	(Pass)
3NT			

Opener has a maximum, with a source of tricks in diamonds, and a half spade stopper himself so he bids 3NT.

There is another possible use for responder's balancing redouble: showing a raise to 2NT with 4-4 in the minors and no spade stopper. Opener then places the contract.

OPENER		RESPONDER	
♠ 10 7 6		♠ 8 3	
♥ A K 7 2		♥ Q 9 3	
♦ K Q J 8		♦ A 10 7 6	
♣ Q 9 3		♣ K 8 4 2	
1NT	(Pass)	2♠	(Double)
Pass	(Pass)	Redouble	(Pass)
3♦	All Pass		

If opener has a spade stopper, he makes his normal bid (2NT = minimum, 3♣ = maximum if you play that; showing interest in 3NT or not opposite a club suit if you play the original version where 2♠ is only a club one-suiter).

They double a 2NT diamond transfer

This will be uncommon, since the response is in notrump. Presumably the double would show a take-out of diamonds, responder's known long suit. Opener can bid 3♣ or 3♦ normally. Redouble should show a good defensive hand, likely with only 2 diamonds. 4-4 in the majors should be implied:

OPENER		RESPONDER	
♠ A K 10 3		♠ 8	
♥ K Q 8 7		♥ J 3	
♦ 10 3		♦ A 9 7 6 5 2	
♣ K J 8		♣ Q 9 6 3	

1NT	(Pass)	2NT	(Double)
Redouble	(3♠)	Double!	

Responder doubles based on opener's redouble and we collect a nice penalty instead of a possible minus, or a partscore in diamonds.

What should a pass mean? I think it should deny a diamond fit and show some interest in defending but otherwise not be specific. If opener does pass the double, then responder's reopening 3♣ bid would be asking for a choice of minors (if the above is agreed to, opener would surely be passing 3♣).

Opponents overcall over a minor transfer

If they overcall responder's suit, they are presumably making a take-out, probably for the majors. Opener's double would show a fit and suitable values for either 3NT or play in the minor.

If they overcall a different suit, opener's double would be for penalty. If he has a good fit for the minor, he can bid 3NT or perhaps another suit, knowing that responder can bail out to 4 of the minor if he has a bad hand.

If an overcall comes back to responder, he can balance with a double to show 'cards' if they are in a major, and penalty if they are in a minor.

A final point about slam bidding without competition

Responder can continue with 4 of his minor to show a slam try but leaving it up to opener. It is important to discuss this as opener might take it as a game invitation.

Responder also needs a Blackwood bid, and I say the cheapest bid over responder's minor should be used. That way a jump to 4NT can be a quantitative raise with perhaps a 5332 hand with 5 in the minor.

OPENER	RESPONDER
1NT	2♠
3♣	4♣: slam try, long clubs, no short suit
	4♦: RKC (Roman Keycard Blackwood) in clubs
	4NT: invitation to slam in either clubs or notrump

4♣ might look like: ♠ K 5
♥ A Q 6
♦ 9 2
♣ K Q 8 7 6 4

4♦ might look like: ♠ 4
♥ K Q 7
♦ K 3
♣ A Q 10 7 6 4 2

4NT might look like: ♠ K 3
♥ K J 4
♦ A 8 6
♣ K J 10 8 5.

Conclusion

Minor suit transfers are a useful thing to play over 1NT. Whether you play the bare-bones basics or the rest of what I propose, be sure to discuss it carefully with partner.

Good luck and enjoy!

3
Flannery

Introduction

Flannery is a popular convention in the USA, being invented by Bill Flannery. It is normally a 2♦ opening, though some use 2♥. The opening normally shows 4 spades and 5 hearts and about 11-15 High Card Points (HCP). I will assume for now we are talking about 2♦ Flannery. The range is limited to 15 HCP on the upper end because with more, you can open 1♥ planning to reverse into 2♠ on the next round, showing 16-21 HCP.

What are the possible advantages of playing Flannery? There are four main ones that come to my mind:

1. If you open 1♥ then raise a 1♠ response to 2♠, it is known that you have exactly 3-card support.
2. There is no necessity for responding 1♠ to a 1♥ opening with a 4-card suit, thus the 1♠ response can show 5+ spades.
3. The 2♦ opening is more preemptive than a 1♥ opening. It is dangerous to overcall at the 3-level, yet not bidding could mean getting 'blown out'.

4. If you have a fit in either major you discover it right out of the box. This is useful if you can blast right to game in either major, perhaps preemptively.

What are the possible disadvantages? The main loss is from not having an alternate use for a 2♦ opening, such as natural weak two, Multi, strong, 3-suiter, etc. The other loss comes from preemption when it is responder rather than the opponents who is being preempted.

Refined parameters for opening Flannery

There have been variations, some of which I will discuss later. For now the main question is: can you open Flannery with more than 4-5 in the majors? This is a thorny issue and I will discuss both ways of playing it. For now, I will assume that only 4-5 is permitted.

The second issue is about evaluation: if you have 15 HCP and strong playing strength, particularly 4-5-4-0 (or 0-4), I suggest upgrading to a 1♥ opening. On the lower end, it is just a matter of how light you want to open the bidding: include bad 11's, or some 10-counts? Up to you.

Responding to 2♦ Flannery

These are the simplest and as far as I know, original responses to 2♦:

Pass: long diamonds, no game interest, no major suit fit
2♥: non-forcing; could be bust with 2 hearts up to a real heart fit just short of an invitation
2♠: non- forcing, like a 2♥ response but 3+ spades
2NT: asking, at least invitational values
3♣: non-forcing, long clubs
3♦: invitational, natural

3♥ or 3♠: real fit, invitational
3NT, 4♥ or 4♠: sign-off

If responder makes an invitational response, opener reevaluates his hand for play in the strain that responder is inviting in. As usual, extra HCP, well-placed honors, a fit (in the case of a 3♦ response), and prime cards are positives.

If responder bids 2♥ or 2♠, opener should pass unless he has solid extras and a 4-card minor. In this case I suggest bidding the 4-card minor to show this hand type. It might even lead to a huge fit that would otherwise be buried.

♠ A J 10 3	♠ 2
♥ A 10 8 7 3	♥ K 2
♦ –	♦ 10 8 7 5
♣ K Q 9 4	♣ A J 10 8 7 6

OPENER	RESPONDER
2♦[1]	2♥[2]
3♣[3]	6♣[4]

(1) Flannery 2♦, showing 11-15 with 4 spades and 5 hearts
(2) non-forcing, at least 2 hearts but less than invitational
(3) 4-card suit, extra values; responder to place the contract
(4) bingo!

♠ A 10 4 3	♠ 7
♥ A K 10 8 7	♥ 9 3
♦ 3	♦ Q J 10 8 7
♣ J 8 7	♣ K Q 9 6 5

OPENER	RESPONDER
2♦	2♥

Responder plays in the known fit rather than gamble a pass of 2♦. Once in a while an opponent will bid 3♦ and responder can double!

Decision to invite game

One problem with Flannery is that responder must decide how high to bid and in spite of the limits of the 2♦ opening, there is a wide range of playing strength that opener can have. Consider this responder hand when partner opens 2♦:

RESPONDER 1
- ♠ K 8 7
- ♥ A 4 3
- ♦ 7 6 5
- ♣ J 10 8 3

Are you worth an invitational 3♥? Consider either hand that opener might have below:

OPENER 1
- ♠ A Q 9 3
- ♥ K Q 6 5 2
- ♦ 3
- ♣ A 9 4

OPENER 1
- ♠ Q 7 5 4
- ♥ K Q J 9 2
- ♦ K 4
- ♣ 9 2

Opposite opener 1, game is excellent and has play for 11 tricks. Opposite opener 2, 3♥ will usually be down, perhaps two. If you were not playing Flannery, you could raise to 2♥ and leave it up to opener, having shown values + a real heart fit. Opener 1 would make a game try of 2♠ or 3♣ and you would bid game. Opener 2 would pass and play in 2♥. This is what I meant when I said Flannery can preempt the responder.

It could be argued that opener 1 should bid again over 2♥, but responder could have this hand:

RESPONDER 2

♠ 8 4
♥ 9 3
♦ J 8 7 6 5
♣ Q 8 6 5

Now you could be going for a big number if you bid again, as responder has neither a fit nor useful values.

There is thus going to be some guesswork involved. I suggest a middle of the road approach, where responder just bids game with a strong invitation, and invites with good single raises or weak invitations. You can adjust according to whether you are playing Matchpoints (where conservatism is often rewarded) or IMPs (where, especially vulnerable, aggression often pays), or your own preferences.

Responding to a 2NT ask

These are the classic replies to a 2NT ask:

2♦ - 2NT
3♣: 3 clubs, i.e. 4-5-1-3
3♦: 3 diamonds, 4-5-3-1
3♥: 4-5-2-2, minimum
3♠: 4-5-2-2, maximum
3NT: 4-5-2-2, maximum, cards in the minor suits
4♣ or 4♦: bidding the 4-card suit with 5440

The theory is that responder is well placed, by knowing opener's shape, where and how high to place the contract. Since 2NT shows at least invitational values, if responder continues with 3♥ or 3♠, opener should go on to game if he has a good hand.

♠ J654   ♠ 32
♥ KQ10 76   ♥ A93
♦ 2   ♦ 986
♣ AJ3   ♣ KQ952

2♦ - 2NT[(1)]
3♣[(2)] **- 4♥**

(1) asking, at least invitational
(2) bidding the shape – 3 clubs so 4-5-1-3

On this deal, where responder has all his strength in one minor, the answer to 2NT tells him the hands fit well. If opener had bid 3♦ instead, responder would bid 3♥, non-forcing. If opener had bid 3♥ (4-5-2-2 minimum), responder would pass. If opener bids higher responder is forced to bid 4♥.

There was never much discussion of slam tools in the original methods that I ever heard about, and this is where there is room for improvement in the responding structure. For the moment I suggest this: if responder bids 2NT and his next bid is 4♣, that shows a slam try in hearts, if his next bid is 4♦ that shows a slam try in spades.

♠ AQ93   ♠ K102
♥ KQ976   ♥ AJ84
♦ 9   ♦ 1076
♣ K87   ♣ AQJ

2♦ - 2NT
3♣ - 4♣[(1)]
4NT - 5♥[(2)]
6♥

(1) slam try in hearts (artificial)
(2) two keycards, no ♥Q

Most of the time responder will land in 4♥, but when he finds opener short in diamonds he knows there is a 'magic fit'. Still, he needs opener to have a good hand so he issues the slam invitation with 4♣ and with a maximum, opener takes over with Roman Keycard Blackwood (RKC).

Note that clubs are the lowest minor suit, and hearts are the lowest major suit. Thus we say that hearts and clubs 'correspond'. In the same way spades and diamonds correspond (both are higher ranking). The use of 4♣ and 4♦ in the suggested way is called 'corresponding minor slam tries'. This might help you remember them if they come up.

Might responder wish that 4♣ was a slam try in clubs instead? He might, but playing the odds, he is more likely to have slam interest in opener's 5-card or 4-card suit than in opener's 3-card or singleton suit.

Opponents compete over Flannery

If the opponents overcall, double is for penalty.

Bidding 3 of a major 2♦ - (3♣) - 3♥ is similar to bidding 3♥ in this auction 1♥ - (3♣) - 3♥. (For clarity, opponents' bids are shown in brackets.)

The 3♣ overcall has taken away the ability to bid 2♥, so responder has to bid 3♥ on reasonable+ 2♥ raises or weak invites. Responder has to overbid and bid game with a full value invitation. Thus, opener might bid game over 3♥ with a maximum.

If an overcall comes back to opener, he should normally pass but can reopen with a double with a void in their suit and some extra values.

If they double 2♦:

2♦ - (Double) - ?

Pass: willing to play in 2♦. I suggest that opener reopen with a redouble if he is void in diamonds; there might be a much better club fit available

Redouble: penalty, and seeks penalty cooperation from opener

other bids: ignore the double

You might prefer to use redouble to solve some of responder's close game try hands.

2♦ - (Double) - Redouble: has mild invitation in a major. Opener bids 2♥ if he wants to stop in 2♥, 2♠ if he wants to stop in 2♠ but wants to get to game in hearts, and opener can just bid 4♥ if he wants to be in either game, counting on responder to correct to 4♠ if that is where the fit is.

Going back to our responder 1 and 2, and opener 1 and 2. If responder has the bad hand (2-2-5-4 with 3 HCP), he bids 2♥ which opener must pass (opener can still bid 3 of a minor with 5440 and a maximum).

If responder has the mild invite (3-3-3-4 with 8 HCP), he redoubles. With the good hand, opener 1 bids 4♥ since he wants to be in game, and responder passes since the fit is in hearts. With the bad hand, opener 2 bids 2♥ and responder passes. Refer to the hands on pages 46 and 47 if you need to refresh your memory of what each player had.

Quiz on basic Flannery

Assume you are using the methods so far discussed (including the extra suggestions I have made). How would these pair of hands be bid? Watch to see if the opponents are bidding.

1.
♠ A Q 9 3	♠ K 8 4
♥ K 7 6 5 4	♥ A Q J 3
♦ J	♦ 9 7 5
♣ Q 7 6	♣ A 10 4

Opponents pass.

2♦	2NT
3♣	4♣
4♥	

Responder could bid 4♥ but decides to give a magic slam a try-out, so he bids 2NT, asking. Opener shows the right shape, 4-5-1-3, by bidding 3♣, so responder bids 4♣, the corresponding minor, to show slam interest in hearts. Opener has a bad hand so he bids 4♥. With a medium hand, opener might bid 4♦ ('Last Train', a topic Eric Rodwell's bidding topics book 1).

2.   ♠ A K 10 4   ♠ J 9 5 3
        ♥ A Q 9 7 6   ♥ K 4
        ♦ 6   ♦ 9 4 3
        ♣ Q 10 3   ♣ K 7 6 5

           2♦   (3♦ overcall)   ?

        2♦   (3♦)   3♠   (Pass)
        4♠

Responder wants to compete to 3♠ once they overcall 3♦. This is a wide range bid but denies a strong invitation. Opener carries to game with a maximum, especially one short in their suit.

3.   ♠ A J 9 4   ♠ 10 5 3
        ♥ A 10 7 6 5   ♥ 2
        ♦ K Q 7 6   ♦ J 8 5 3
        ♣ –   ♣ A 10 7 6 5

Opponents pass.

2♦ - 2♠
3♦ - Pass

Opener bids 3♦ to show 4-5-4-0 and a good hand. Responder is relieved to find a playable fit and 'gets out of Dodge' by passing.

4.
♠ J 9 6 5	♠ K 3
♥ A J 8 6 5	♥ Q 10 4
♦ Q 3	♦ K 8 7
♣ K J	♣ 10 9 7 6 5

2♦   (Double)   ?

2♦   (Double)   Redouble   (Pass)
2♥

Responder redoubles to show a mild game try in a major, and opener bids 2♥ to show no interest in a heart game. Responder passes, having a fit in hearts.

How Flannery affects sequences when you open 1♥

Some just play that a 1♠ response shows 5+spades, period. This is simple but leaves us with some problems. First of all, if the opening is 1♥ with 4-6 in the majors, how do we find a 4-4 spade fit? It isn't usually important if responder has 2 or more hearts as we have an 8-card fit there as well, but this is a problem if responder is short in hearts.

It was suggested to me once that a 1♠ response should show 5+ spades, or a hand with 4 spades and 0 or 1 heart. This solves some of the problems:

OPENER	RESPONDER 1
♠ Q 8 7 6	♠ J 9 4 3
♥ K Q J 9 4 3	♥ 10 2
♦ A 3	♦ J 8 7 6
♣ 9	♣ A J 8

1♥	1NT
2♥	

Responder 1 bids 1NT, since opener has 4 spades only if he also has 6 hearts.

OPENER	RESPONDER 2
♠ Q 8 7 6	♠ A J 10 4
♥ K Q J 9 4 3	♥ 2
♦ A 3	♦ K 8 7
♣ 9	♣ J 6 5 4 2

1♥	1♠
3♠	4♠

Responder 2 bids 1♠ since he is short in hearts. Opener has to jump to show the 4th trump and playing potential, since a raise to 2♠ shows exactly 3-card support.

A 1♠ response is also possible on a 4-card suit in two other situations:

1. the suit is strong, suitable for a 4-3 fit, or
2. responder is worried about missing game if opener is 4-6 in the majors. Responder 2 would have this concern if he had a second heart as well as with his actual hand.

Opener is supposed to raise a 1♠ response with 3-card support, but with xxx and 6 quality hearts, I recommend a 2♥ rebid.

Opening Flannery with 4-6 or 5-6

Some prefer this solution:

2♦	2♥
3♥: 4-6, invitational;	
don't bid this with	
a bad minimum	
2♦	2♠
3♠: 5-6, invitational	

Of course if this is allowed, new responses to 2NT are needed. How about this?

2♦	2NT

3♣: minimum, 4-5
3♦: maximum, 4-5, not 4-5-2-2
3♥: 4-6 minimum
3♠: 4-6 maximum
3NT: 4-5-2-2 maximum
4♣ or 4♦: 4-card suit with 5440
4♥: 5-6 in the majors

If opener shows a minimum with 4-5, responder can sign off in 3 of a major, or bid 3♦ to ask for opener's shape:

2♦	2NT
3♣	3♦: what is your side
	shape with your
	minimum 4-5?
3♥: 4-5-1-3	
3♠: 4-5-3-1	
3NT: 4-5-2-2	

♠ A J 8 6	♠ 2
♥ K 10 9 4 3	♥ Q J
♦ K 8 7	♦ A Q J 9 4 3
♣ 2	♣ A 8 6 5

2♦	2NT[1]
3♣ [2]	3♦ [3]
3♠ [4]	?

(1) must bid 2NT as opener might have 6 hearts
(2) minimum, 4-5
(3) asking again
(4) 2nd step = 3 diamonds, so 4-5-3-1

Now responder wants to bid RKC in diamonds, opener's 3-card suit. I suggest that 4NT by responder, after bidding 2NT, is RKC in opener's 3-card minor (diamonds if opener shows 2-2 in the minors). On this deal responder would continue with 4NT and opener would bid 5♥ to show 2 diamond keycards without the ♦Q, and responder bids 6♦.

If opener shows a maximum with 4-5 (not 4-5-2-2) by bidding 3♦, we are in a game force. Thus, responder can bid 3♥ to ask for the 3-card minor.

2♦	2NT
3♦	3♥: what is your 3-card minor?
3♠: clubs	
3NT: diamonds	

Note that since we are in a game force (since 3♦ showed a maximum), responder can bid 3♠ to set spades as trump and doesn't need to use 4♦, the 'corresponding minor' convention.

If opener showed 4-6 in the majors and a minimum by bidding 3♥, I suggest that we are in a game force unless responder passes

3♥. 3♠ could then be used to ask for the 2 (or 3) card minor. This might help us bid a magic slam.

2♦	2NT
3♥	3♠: what is your longer minor?
3NT: clubs	
4♣: diamonds	

Corresponding minor can be used if opener bids 3NT. If opener bids 4♣, I suggest 4♦ = slam try in hearts and 4NT is RKC in spades.

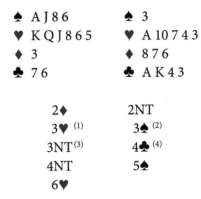

♠ A J 8 6	♠ 3
♥ K Q J 8 6 5	♥ A 10 7 4 3
♦ 3	♦ 8 7 6
♣ 7 6	♣ A K 4 3

2♦	2NT
3♥ (1)	3♠ (2)
3NT(3)	4♣ (4)
4NT	5♠
6♥	

(1) 4-6 in the majors, minimum
(2) asking for the longer minor
(3) step 1 = longer clubs
(4) corresponding minor = slam try in hearts

With a 'maximum minimum', opener bids RKC into 6♥.

More twists

Still want some more 'twists' to play with Flannery? Here are some more suggestions. If responder bids 2♥ and you have 5-6 in the majors, rebid 2NT.

2♦   2♥

2NT: 5-6 in the majors; responder can bid 3♣ as a 're-try' to see if you truly have a maximum

If the opponents overcall 3 of a minor and it passed back around to opener:

2♦   (3♣)   Pass   (Pass)

Double: 4-6 in the majors; not a bad minimum
3♦: 4-5-4-0
3♥: 5-6 in the majors

If the opponents compete over a 2NT response:

2♦   (Pass)   2NT   (3♣)

Double: at least 3 clubs; if clubs are Jxx or worse, some defensive values
Pass: the normal bid with 4-5 (other than double)
3♦: 4-5-4-0
3♥ or 3♠: normal (4-6 in the majors)
4♥: normal (5-6 in the majors)

If opener passes it back to responder, he knows that opener is 4-5 and can't double 3♣. Responder can double 3♣ for penalty, bid 3 of a major invitational, or 4 of a minor 'corresponding minor' convention. I see no reason that a balancing 3♦ shouldn't be natural and game forcing.

♠ A K 7 5   ♠ 3 2
♥ Q 10 5 4 3 ♥ A 8 7
♦ 2   ♦ A K J 8 3
♣ Q 6 2   ♣ A 7 3

2♦	(Pass)	2NT	(3♣)
Double			

The penalty should be considerable.

A 3♦ response can be used to show a forcing hand with a long minor. This is more likely than a hand that is exactly invitational with diamonds. It requests a 3♥ reply:

2♦ - 3♦: game forcing, has own long minor
3♥ forced, whereafter:
- 3♠: has clubs
- 3NT: has diamonds, non-forcing
- 4♣: has diamonds, wants to be in at least 5♦

Opener can support responder's minor at the 4-level without a good fit (if responder needed a good fit he would ask with 2NT), provided he has useful outside cards.

I suggest that 4♠ be used as RKC in the minor.

♠ A 7 5 4   ♠ 2
♥ K Q J 8 7 ♥ A 2
♦ K   ♦ A Q J 10 7 6 5 4
♣ 7 6 3   ♣ A 2

2♦ - 3♦: has own long minor, game forcing
3♥ - 4♣: big hand, long diamonds, too strong/unsuitable for 3NT
4♦ - 4♠: RKC in diamonds
5♦ - 5♠: showing all the key values, inviting 7
7NT

Opener cooperates with 4♦ but doesn't bid 4♠ RKC since he lacks a club control.

I suggest that if opener is 4-6 in the majors, he can bid 3♥ if his hand is OK for at least one minor. Otherwise, opener bids 3♠ to show 4-6 in the majors, and 3NT to show 5-6 in the majors. Bidding is natural after that (4NT is RKC in hearts).

Defending against Flannery

If you want something simple, Double = diamonds, and a 2♥ over-call = take-out (might have spades also or just minors).

Versus 2♦ Flannery, they are probably not in a playable contract so many use double to show values, about 13-15 HCP.

$$(2♦) \qquad ?$$

Double: 13–15 HCP or a strong hand

2♥: take-out (opener has 5+ hearts); might be just minors or the ability to play in spades also

2♠ or 3♠: natural; 3♠ is 'strong', inviting a raise

2NT: 16-19 HCP, natural

3♣ or 3♦: natural overcalls, reasonable hand for the vulnerability

3♥: has long good minor suit, seeks a heart stopper for 3NT. Partner can bid 4♣, 'pass or correct', if weak and lacking a heart stopper. This allows an out in 4 of the long minor. Can also bid 4NT to ask for the minor at the 5-level

In response, a bid in hearts is a cuebid and a spade bid is natural. Over a 2NT overcall I suggest:

$$(2♦) \qquad 2NT \qquad (Pass) \qquad ?$$

3♣ or 3♦: weak, natural

3♥: transfer to spades. The 2NT bidder might jump to 4♠ with
   a suitable fit
3♠: forces 3NT to bid a long minor for a slam try

If you start with double, and you have 13-15 HCP, you are leaving further action to partner. If you double with a strong hand, you are planning to bid again freely.

Quiz

How might these hands be bid after RHO opens 2♦ Flannery?

(2♦) - ? - (2♥) - ?

♠ K 8 7	♠ A 2
♥ J 8 7	♥ 9 2
♦ A Q J 3	♦ 9 4 2
♣ K 9 3	♣ Q J 10 8 7 6

Answer:

(2♦)   Double   (2♥)   3♣.

This allows 'advancer' (partner of the double) to compete to 3♣ without overstating his values. If the double showed diamonds, then we might never get in: it is dangerous for the 4333 hand to balance later, and if he passes and partner overcalls 3♣, he will expect a better hand and bid over 3♣.

If an opponent uses 2♦ for something else (maybe Multi), then they might use a 2♥ opening as Flannery. In this case they are in a playable contract so Double = take-out and other bids are as against a 2♦ Flannery opening.

Conclusion

Flannery is a popular convention that definitely has some merit. It is worth considering some of the finer aspects of it, as addressed in this chapter, if you want to play it.

This chapter is also useful for those who don't want to play it but want to understand it's use by opponents. To this end also a defense against Flannery was included.

4
Bidding in Fourth Position

Introduction

Bidding in fourth position ('seat') is a term that could apply to an almost endless number of auctions, where it is your turn to bid after partner and RHO (Right Hand Opponent) have passed. This bidding situation is also referred to as 'balancing'. However, I am limiting this topic to a discussion of 1-of-a-suit – Pass – Pass to you. That will be a fairly meaty topic as it is.

When RHO opens, say, 1♦, and you have a hand like these below:

1. ♠ A K 8 3
   ♥ K 2
   ♦ Q 10 2
   ♣ J 8 7 6

2. ♠ A 2
   ♥ Q 8 7
   ♦ A 8 7
   ♣ K 8 7 6 5

3. ♠ K 8 6 5 4
   ♥ K 2
   ♦ 8 7
   ♣ J 9 4 3

None of the above hands is suited to direct action, though some would try an overcall of 1♠ in 1, 2♣ in 2, or 1♠ in 3. This might depend on the vulnerability. But when a 1♦ opening is passed around

LHO	Partner	RHO	You
1♦	Pass	Pass	?

you either take action or the contract is 1♦. You can't wait and see if partner will bid because he has already declined to do so. It is common knowledge that balancing bids can be lighter than direct seat bids, but how much lighter? How do you follow them up?

Balancing with 1NT

One of the most common balancing bids is 1NT, which has a wider, and weaker, range than a direct 1NT overcall. The lower limit is about 10-11 HCP (High Card Points) and the upper limit would vary according to agreement. Some have theorized that a balancing 1NT over a minor should have a higher minimum than over a major because there are more options to bid a suit at the 1-level.

If this appeals to you then fine, but I suggest for simplicity keeping the range approximately the same over minor and major openings. Also, I don't want to have to balance on a weak 4-card suit when 1NT seems more descriptive.

I recommend a range of 11-15 for a balancing 1NT. I do suggest that when the opening is a major that most 16's be included in the 1NT range since there is less chance of being able to balance with a Double then rebid 1NT when the opening is a major. Thus:

LHO	Partner	RHO	You
1♣	Pass	Pass	1NT = 11–15
1♠	Pass	Pass	1NT = 11–16

Of course just because you have the right point count does not mean that 1NT is the right bid, even if you are balanced. If you have a weak doubleton in their suit then a take-out double (or overcall) is normally preferred unless those alternatives seem worse. One thing that a balancing 1NT bid does NOT promise is a stopper in opener's suit. Reopening the bidding with a balanced 11 HCP means you are playing partner for a reasonable hand and hopefully some strength in their suit.

As always, vulnerability and playing strength matter. Would you balance with 1NT on the hands below? Does vulnerability (or form of scoring, i.e. matchpoints versus IMPs) matter?

LHO	PARTNER	RHO	YOU
1♣	Pass	Pass	?

1.	♠ A Q 8 7	2.	♠ K J	3.	♠ A 9	4.	♠ A Q 8
	♥ K 9 3		♥ A 8 7 6		♥ Q 8 6 5 4		♥ K J 9
	♦ Q 10 7 6		♦ K 10 7 6		♦ 9 7 6		♦ Q J 9 3
	♣ K 9		♣ 9 5 4		♣ A J 3		♣ 6 5 4

Hand 1 could double, or bid 1NT. This is mainly a matter of personal preference. With the desire to show a reasonable balanced hand, and protect the vulnerable Kx of clubs, I prefer 1NT. However it is also a perfectly normal takeout double so it is close.

Hand 2 either balances with 1NT or perhaps 1♦ on the weak 4-card suit. Pass of course is also possible. If I was vulnerable I might prefer to bid 1♦ and hope for the best but 1NT would be the systemic bid if you choose to bid at all.

Hand 3 should balance with 1♥. You can hopefully get to notrump later if you belong there.

Hand 4 is an ideal 1NT balance, albeit with no club stopper. The hand is too flat for a balancing double in my opinion and is strong enough to risk bidding 1NT.

Balancing with a 1-level overcall

These can definitely be light, and can be 4-card suits, especially if you want to avoid bidding a light 1NT when vulnerable. It is obviously preferable to have a reasonable 4-card suit.

One factor to consider: length in opener's suit. If you have four or more cards there, then the odds that they are in a 6-card (or less) fit is greater. Even so, they often can make seven tricks and with anything reasonable for offence you want to fight for the contract. The main danger with hands with length in their suit, and moderate values, is that they can make something (game perhaps) in a different suit.

I had this hand recently playing with a partner who is adamant about making light balances with a 5-card major:

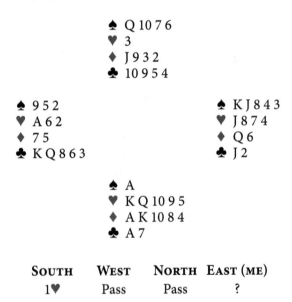

♠ Q 10 7 6
♥ 3
♦ J 9 3 2
♣ 10 9 5 4

♠ 9 5 2
♥ A 6 2
♦ 7 5
♣ K Q 8 6 3

♠ K J 8 4 3
♥ J 8 7 4
♦ Q 6
♣ J 2

♠ A
♥ K Q 10 9 5
♦ A K 10 8 4
♣ A 7

SOUTH	WEST	NORTH	EAST (ME)
1♥	Pass	Pass	?

I think it is right to pass with such a weak hand and four hearts. However, in an effort to keep partnership harmony, I balanced with 1♠. The bidding continued:

SOUTH	WEST	NORTH	EAST
1♥	Pass	Pass	1♠
2♦	2♣	3♦	Pass
3♠	Double*	3NT	All Pass

*Double requests NOT a spade lead, and with hearts and diamonds bid by the opponents, implies interest in a club lead.

I dutifully (again) led the ♣J to the ace. Declarer dropped the ♦Q in two rounds then crossed to hand to lead a heart to the king (playing the 10 lets him make easily). He finished one down for a nervous +100.

Our teammates bid it this way:

SOUTH	NORTH
2♣	2♦
2♥	2♠*
3♦	4♦
6♦	

*Forced response (2♥ was 'Kokish', showing hearts or a game forcing balanced hand).

Yikes! East did not lead a club so now North dropped the ♦Q and led the ♥10 from dummy. This was a necessary play as he needed three heart tricks for club pitches from hand. It didn't matter whether West won or ducked the heart, +1370!

In any event, balancing overcalls are like normal overcalls in terms of the upper limit, they just can be weaker on the lower end. Partner tries to bid normally over them but pulls it in a notch when it is close.

LHO	PARTNER	RHO	YOU
1♦	Pass	Pass	?

1. ♠ A K J 8 3   2. ♠ A K Q 2   3. ♠ K J 8 3 2   4. ♠ A K 10 8 7
   ♥ A 2   ♥ 9 8 7   ♥ Q 3   ♥ 2
   ♦ 10 2   ♦ 7 5 3   ♦ 9 4   ♦ A 8 3
   ♣ K 9 4 3   ♣ J 8 7   ♣ J 8 6 5   ♣ K Q J 8

The first hand, though strong, is not enough to double then bid spades so just bid 1♠.

The second hand would probably not bid in direct seat (unless you are nonvulnerable and quite aggressive) but can sensibly balance with 1♠. Of course any time you balance with a hand you wouldn't bid with in direct seat there is no guarantee that it will work well.

The third hand should make a light balance of 1♠, nonvulnerable especially. The odds are that partner has something like an opening hand but not suited to bidding directly. Perhaps he has this hand:

♠ Q 9
♥ A 10 7 6
♦ K 2
♣ A 10 7 4 3

Some would overcall 2♣ but I don't like 2 of a minor overcalls with broken 5-card suits. Passing would be a popular choice, hoping to back in with a 2-suiter double if the response is 1♠.

Now that 1♦ has been passed around to you, bidding 1♠ protects partner's hand.

The last hand is too strong for 1♠ in direct seat (by my lights; not all experts would agree with that) so start by doubling then bidding spades in the reopening seat.

I would say that doubling then bidding a suit should be a bit lighter than in direct seat to help narrow the range. Consider these hands:

♠ A J 9 8 3
♥ A K 3
♦ K 2
♣ Q 9 3

or

♠ A 2
♥ K Q 10 6 5
♦ 8 3
♣ A K 5 3

Neither hand is quite good enough to double then bid your suit in my opinion (I think most experts would agree). Partner will normally respond to an overcall with 8 HCP which is what you would need to want to be in game (partner can of course respond with less if he can raise, or has good shape).

I would recommend doubling then bidding the major with both hands in reopening seat. This allows partner to pass a reopening overcall with a flat 8, or nondescript 9, HCP.

Balancing with a double

A double shows either a strong hand (as just noted, perhaps not quite as strong a hand as it would show in direct seat), or at least three cards in any unbid major. The question is how light can you be?

Again it is a matter of preference but I would say if you have perfect shape, which would be 4441 short in their suit, you might have as little as 6 HCP. With a doubleton, as little as 8 HCP.

This is substantially weaker than in direct seat so responses will have to be a bit different. A full deal might be like this:

♠ J 7 6 2
♥ Q 3
♦ 8 3 2
♣ 9 7 5 4

♠ K 9   ♠ A 10 8 4
♥ A 8 6 2   ♥ J 10 9 7
♦ A 10 7 5   ♦ 6
♣ Q 10 6   ♣ J 8 3 2

♠ Q 5 3
♥ K 5 4
♦ K Q J 9 4
♣ A K

SOUTH	WEST	NORTH	EAST
1♦	Pass	Pass	?

1♦ would likely make. You can easily make a heart partial and have a shot at 10 tricks.

Reopening 2-level overcalls

Obviously balancing at the 2-level with a 4-card suit is out. Weak 5-card suits should be avoided also, if possible. Lean toward bidding 1NT or double as these bids are more flexible.

LHO	PARTNER	RHO	YOU
1♠	Pass	Pass	?

1. ♠ 9 4 3
   ♥ K 8 6 5 4
   ♦ A J 8
   ♣ K 3

2. ♠ 9 3
   ♥ K 9 2
   ♦ A J 7 6 5
   ♣ K 9 3

3. ♠ A 2
   ♥ 9 3 2
   ♦ J 2
   ♣ K J 10 8 4 3

4. ♠ 8
   ♥ A K Q 10 3
   ♦ 9 2
   ♣ J 8 6 5 4

Hand 1 should balance with 1NT. Bidding 2♥ would be a serious mistake in my opinion. Partner could easily have a hand like :

♠ Q J x x
♥ x
♦ K 9 x x
♣ Q J 10 x.

Hand 2 could balance with Double, 1NT, or 2♦. Again, the worst is bidding 2♦ on a mediocre 5-card suit and a flat hand. I prefer Double but 1NT is OK.

Hand 3 could balance with 1NT, trading on the 6-card minor but it seems more normal to balance with 2♣.

Hand 4 screams to bid hearts. You could balance with 2♠, which would still be a Michaels cuebid but I think you are a touch light for that and prefer 2♥.

Higher level balances

1. A balancing jump overcall is 'intermediate' – good 6-card suit and about 12-15 HCP. This is one way to narrow the range of a balancing overcall.

Opener	Partner	RHO	You
1♥	Pass	Pass	?

1. ♠ A Q 10 7 6 5   2. ♠ A 2
   ♥ A 2   ♥ K 8 7
   ♦ 9 2   ♦ 8
   ♣ K 10 3   ♣ K Q 9 7 6 5 4

Hand 1 is a perfect 2♠ bid, intermediate.
Hand 2 seems just right for 3♣.

2. A balancing **cuebid** is Michaels, showing the same suits
    that it would in direct seat.

Opener	Partner	RHO	You
1♠	Pass	Pass	2♠: spades and a minor

Of course if you play a cuebid as something else ('top and bottom' or whatever) then that would apply in reopening seat as well.

Just as in direct seat, it shows something to force to the 3-level, and a bit more when vulnerable. These hands would be suitable for a 2♠ balance:

♠ 2
♥ A Q 10 8 7
♦ K 9 7 5 4 3
♣ 2

♠ A
♥ K J 9 6 5
♦ K J 9 3 2
♣ 9 2

Of course you could be stronger.

3. A balancing **2NT** shows a strong balanced hand. It is NOT
    an unusual notrump. I suggest a range of 19-20 (or bad 21).

Opener	Partner	RHO	You
1♠	Pass	Pass	?

1. ♠ A Q 3
    ♥ K 9
    ♦ A Q 9 7 6
    ♣ K J 8

2. ♠ A 2
    ♥ A J 10 8
    ♦ A K 3
    ♣ K 9 7 6

Hand 1 is an ideal 2NT balance. This shows more than it takes to double then bid notrump (about 17-18 or perhaps a good 16).

Hand 2 could double, but I prefer 2NT to show the values. Partner can bid Stayman or use a Jacoby transfer to try to get to hearts.

Responding to a balancing overcall

Balancing bids have wider ranges than normal so it is not possible to be as accurate in responding to them. I suggest taking the approach that you might miss an occasional game in the interest of not bidding too much ('hanging partner') when partner might be light.

That being said, we want to try to have good bidding. I said earlier that responding to overcalls with 8 HCP is normal, but you might want to bump that up to 9 HCP for a response (say) of 1NT. Instead of a range of 8–11 a 1NT response could then show about 9–12.

RHO	You	LHO	Partner
1♦	Pass	Pass	1♥
Pass	?		

1.	♠ A J 3	2.	♠ K 9 5 4	3.	♠ A Q 9 4
	♥ 9 2		♥ 9 5		♥ J 9
	♦ K 9 7 6		♦ Q 9 5		♦ K Q 9 3
	♣ A 9 6 5		♣ Q J 8 6		♣ Q 8 3

Hand 1 should bid 1NT. You would bid 2NT (perhaps depending on how light you overcall) to a direct seat overcall but over a balancing 1♥, give partner some slack and bid 1NT.

Hand 2 would normally respond 1NT but I suggest passing to narrow the range of the 1NT response a bit.

Hand 3 is too good for 1NT and bids 2NT. This is strongly invitational (good 12-14).

Similarly, raises should probably be a point heavier. A cuebid response normally shows 10 support points; I suggest having 11 or more. A raise shows 7-10 support points. Of course hand evaluation should enter into any close decision.

OPENER	YOU	LHO	PARTNER
1♦	Pass	Pass	1♠
Pass	?		

4. ♠ K 8 7	5. ♠ 9 4 3	6. ♠ A Q 3
♥ A J 8 7	♥ K J 8 4	♥ 9 2
♦ 10 8 7	♦ 9 7 6	♦ A J 8 7 6
♣ Q 10 3	♣ Q 9 8	♣ J 10 3

Hand 4 should raise to 2♠. I would cuebid if partner overcalled directly.

Hand 5 should pass 1♠ (raise a direct overcall).

Hand 6 is a cuebid in either case but has only a little extra opposite a reopening overcall. If partner rebids 2♠, let him out by passing.

Responding to a reopening double

I suggest making more non-jump responses. A jump in a major should show something like 11-13 HCP with a 4-card suit. Jumping can be somewhat weaker with a 5-card suit. A jump to 2NT shows a good 11-13 (maybe a bad 14).

Jumping in a minor should show a 5-card suit and 10-13 HCP.

OPENER	YOU	LHO	PARTNER
1♦	Pass	Pass	Double
Pass	?		

1. ♠ K 2	2. ♠ A J 8 4	3. ♠ K J 8	4. ♠ K 10 3
♥ J 9 7 6 3	♥ K 3	♥ 9 7 6	♥ A 4 3
♦ 9 2	♦ 9 7 6	♦ A 2	♦ A Q 8 3
♣ K Q 9 2	♣ K 10 5 4	♣ K J 6 5 4	♣ 9 6 5

Hand 1 has only 9 HCP but a 5-card suit and good shape. Jump to 2♥.

Hand 2 is also a jump, to 2♠.

Hand 3 could jump to 2NT but NT could easily be better from partner's side so I favor a jump to 3♣.

Hand 4 jumps to 2NT.

As you can see, these jumps are strongly encouraging.

When the response is non-jump, takeout doubler can raise with a fit, perhaps more aggressively than you normally would:

♠ A K 9 3
♥ A 10 3
♦ 9 2
♣ Q J 4 3

Opener	Partner	RHO	You
1♦	Pass	Pass	Double
Pass	1♠	Pass	?

Even if you would normally pass 1♠, you should raise to 2♠ here. Partner might have ♠Q 8 x x ♥K x ♦x x x x ♣A 10 x for example.

A cuebid followup by doubler can be a bit weaker than normal, and partner just assumes he has a good raise to the 2-level, unless he hears otherwise. Change the clubs in the above hand to KQxx and it is just good enough to come back with a 2♦ cuebid.

2♣ range ask after a balancing 1NT

A wide range bid, like 1NT that has a range of 11-15 or 11-16 (and might be bid on 10 HCP) is going to lead to some guesswork. In general, responder should not be too aggressive in trying for game. A 2♣ response, instead of being Stayman in the strict sense, is a 'range finder'.

OPENER	YOU	LHO	PARTNER
1♠	Pass	Pass	1NT
Pass	2♣	Pass	?

- 2NT shows a maximum NT, about 14-16. Does not say anything about unbid major(s).
- 2♦ or 2♥ are normal Stayman responses but show a minimum notrump. Maximum of 13 HCP. Of course there is no need to show a 4-card spade suit.

Over 2NT, you can ask for majors with 3♣. Partner bids 3♦ with no major, and bids an unbid major naturally.

Suppose these are the hands:

YOU	PARTNER
♠ A 10 3	♠ K 9 4
♥ A J 8 7	♥ K 2
♦ 9 2	♦ A 10 4 3
♣ Q 9 7 6	♣ K J 8 3

(1♠)	Pass	1NT
	2♣	2NT
	3♣	3♦
	3NT	

With a reasonable 11 HCP it is worth the risk to try for a game that could easily be cold, so bid 2♣ 'range finder'. With 14 HCP partner shows a maximum by bidding 2NT. You ask for unbid majors by bidding 3♣ and over 3♦ (no unbid major) you sign off in 3NT.

If partner shows a weaker hand by bidding 2♦ or a new major, you can bid appropriately. Over 2♥, I would raise to 3♥ since I like my values and partner could have 13 HCP (it is a bit pushy; pass is fine too). Over 2♦ showing a minimum I would bid 2NT, a sign-off.

If you want a 'twist', here it is: bidding 2♣ then following with a 2-level cuebid shows game interest. Returning to 2NT is a sign-off. Improve the responding hand a bit, to this:

♠ A 10 3
♥ A Q 9 2
♦ 9 2
♣ Q 9 4 3

and you still have game interest over 2♦. Cuebid 2♠ to show some interest in game. Returning to 2NT over 2♦ would be a sign-off.

Responding to a reopening jump overcall

I suggest 2NT, if available, is forcing one round. A raise is a weaker raise, while a cuebid is a stronger game try. A new suit is forcing and natural.

You	Partner
♠ A 10 4	♠ 8
♥ 10	♥ K Q 9 7 6 5 4
♦ A J 8 7	♦ K 9 2
♣ Q 10 7 6 2	♣ A 3

(1♣)	Pass	2♥
	2NT	4♥

If you jump to 3NT partner would probably pull to 4♥ but this makes it easier.

Responding to a reopening 2NT

This one is pretty easy — pretend they opened a weak two bid and partner overcalled 2NT. Most pairs play nothing more complicated than 3♣ is Stayman and Jacoby transfers. If the opening was a major, then 3♠ could show both minors.

Further competition and summary

By now we've run out of time, but you can use normal methods you would after direct seat overcalls and take-out doubles. Just make the advances (i.e. bids in reply to partner's double or overcall) a little sounder to compensate for a possibly weak balancing bid.

I hope you enjoyed this chapter, and good luck!

♪
Smolen

Introduction

Smolen is a convention used over 1NT or 2NT openings to show 5-4 in the majors and a game forcing (GF) hand. It was perhaps created by the late Mike Smolen but in any event bears his name. The basic principle is simple—bid Stayman—opener bids 2♦ (3♦ if the opening was 2NT) to deny a major—then you bid 3 of your FOUR-card major:

1NT	2♣
2♦	3♥: Smolen, showing a GF hand with 5 SPADES and 4 hearts

What is the value of Smolen? It is normally good to have the lead coming up to the balanced hand (especially when it is a strong balanced hand). This is one reason Jacoby transfers are such a good convention. Think of Smolen as a 'delayed transfer' bid. If opener has a 3-card fit (having denied 4 already with the 2♦ bid), he supports the major:

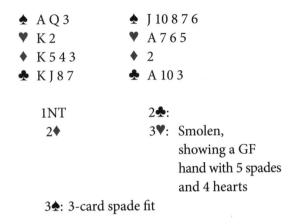

♠ A Q 3	♠ J 10 8 7 6
♥ K 2	♥ A 7 6 5
♦ K 5 4 3	♦ 2
♣ K J 8 7	♣ A 10 3

1NT	2♣:
2♦	3♥: Smolen, showing a GF hand with 5 spades and 4 hearts
3♠: 3-card spade fit	
	4♠

4♠ is a better contract than 3NT, and it is better played from opener's side so the benefits of Smolen can clearly be seen.

If opener has only a 2-card fit for responder's 5-card major, he bids 3NT.

♠ J 8 7	♠ K 9 4 3
♥ K 3	♥ A J 9 7 6
♦ A Q 9 8	♦ J 3
♣ K Q 7 6	♣ 9 4

1NT	2♣
2♦	3♠: Smolen, showing 5 hearts and 4 Spades
3NT	

3NT is not laydown but it is clearly the best game contract. Smolen works the same way when the opening is 2NT. This time the 3♥ or 3♠ bid will not be a jump:

♠ A Q 3	♠ 10 9 7 6 5
♥ K Q 3	♥ J 10 8 7
♦ A 4 3	♦ 5
♣ K Q 8 7	♣ A 9 3

2NT	3♣
3♦	3♥: Smolen, showing 5 spades
3♠	4♠

Responder bids Smolen then tries for slam

Responder can also have a strong enough hand to consider a slam. If opener supports the major at the 3-level – 3♠ – responder can cuebid at the 4-level, or bid 4NT as Roman Keycard Blackwood (RKC) in spades. If responder does cuebid, opener can look at both his values (minimum or maximum), and the 'quality' of his values. It is best to have his 'soft' cards (queens/jacks and to a lesser degree, kings) in the major suits.

♠ K Q 3	♠ A J 9 7 6
♥ K Q 3	♥ A J 8 7
♦ A Q 10 8 7	♦ K J 3
♣ 9 3	♣ 2

1NT	2♣
2♦	3♥
3♠	4♣: cuebid, showing a club control
4NT	5♥
6♠	

Responder's try for slam is aggressive, but opener doesn't have to take over unless he knows he has the right hand.

Playing 3NT with a 5-3 major suit fit

Usually the 5-3 fit will play better, but some hands just seem to call for 3NT even with 3-card support. Having 'soft' double stoppers in the minors, and especially with a weak 3-card holding in the 4-card major, suggests 3NT.

♠ Q 10 3	♠ K J 9 5 2
♥ 10 8 7	♥ Q 6 5 4
♦ A Q J	♦ 2
♣ A Q 9 4	♣ K 10 5

1NT	2♣
2♦	3♥
3NT	

3NT is clearly better than 4♠. The only real downside of bidding 3NT is if responder has a slam try, not knowing about the fit could lead him to undervalue his hand.

If opener bids 3♠ over a 3♥ Smolen bid, responder might bid 3NT. This is natural unless you agree otherwise, but is only a suggestion that opener can overrule and go back to 4♠.

♠ J 10 3	♠ K Q 8 7 6
♥ A 2	♥ Q 10 4 3
♦ A K 8 3	♦ Q 2
♣ K 9 5 3	♣ Q 8

1NT	2♣
2♦	3♥
3♠	3NT

With 5-4-2-2 and values in the minors, responder offers 3NT and opener has the hand to accept notrump.

Playing in the 5-2 major suit fit

Opener can have strong 2-card support for the 5-card major, with a weak minor and be tempted to play the 5-2. This is an awkward judgment to make because responder might have a weak major and length and strength in opener's weak minor. On balance opener should avoid making this decision arbitrarily. Opener might bid 3♠ over 3♥ Smolen with a strong doubleton, possibly reevaluating if responder bids 3NT.

The strongest candidate for just parking it in 4 of the major is with xx in a minor, meaning a 'funny NT' with 6322 and a 6-card minor:

♠ K Q 3	♠ A 10 8 7
♥ K Q	♥ A 9 6 5 4
♦ 10 2	♦ K 3
♣ A Q 10 8 7 6	♣ J 5

1NT	2♣
2♦	3♠
4♥	

4♥ is hardly laydown, but it has better play than 3NT. Note that responder might have

♠ A J x x ♥ 10 x x x x ♦ K Q 9 ♣ J making 3NT a lot better so this is a risky position to take.

Bidding Smolen with 6-4 in the majors

It is quite possible to forget about the 4-card major with 6-4, and this is advisable on most hands that have a strong 6-card major.

♠ 8 7 3	♠ Q J 10 9 4 2
♥ A 9 5 4	♥ K 10 6 2
♦ A K J 3	♦ Q 2
♣ K 2	♣ 10

1NT	4♥: Texas transfer bid
4♠	

Obviously finding a heart fit wouldn't be good on this deal. If responder has a weaker 6-card major and a stronger 4-card major, the odds can change:

♠ K 2	♠ Q 9 6 5 4 3
♥ K 8 6 5	♥ A Q J 9
♦ K Q 3	♦ J 4
♣ K Q 7 6	♣ 2

1NT	2♣
2♥	4♥

The strong 4-4 fit allows the spades to be ruffed out. Even so, a 4-1 heart split will make things awkward. Another reason to bid Smolen with 6-4 is with a slam try:

♠ K J 9	♠ A Q 10 8 7 6
♥ A 2	♥ K J 10 6
♦ A 8 6 5	♦ K 3
♣ A 7 6 4	♣ 2

1NT	2♣
2♦	3♥
3♠	4♣
4NT	5♦
5♥	6♦
6♥	7♠

This is a difficult hand to bid to a grand slam. Over the 4♣ slam try, opener takes over with magic cards. Responder shows 1 keycard, then the trump Q and ♦K. When opener tries with 6♥, responder figures the 6th trump + the ♥K is enough. Opener can't provide any more values than he actually has so responder should sign off with the ♥K and 5422. It is automatic for responder to bid 7♠ with the above hand if the hearts were KQxx instead of KJ10x.

6-4 in the majors with no slam interest

Once opener has denied a 4-card major, it is common to play that a jump to 4♦ or 4♥ are 'delayed Texas', i.e. delayed transfer bids:

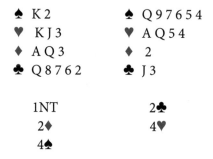

♠ K 2	♠ Q 9 7 6 5 4
♥ K J 3	♥ A Q 5 4
♦ A Q 3	♦ 2
♣ Q 8 7 6 2	♣ J 3

1NT	2♣
2♦	4♥
4♠	

Once opener bids 2♦, responder wants to sign off in 4♠, but as usual he wants to transfer it. Jumping to 'one under' 4 of the long major is a transfer and opener must accept by bidding 4♠. 4♠

needs a lucky trump layout, but it is much better if opener plays it and gets a diamond lead.

QUIZ

Partner opens 1NT. What is your bidding plan with the hands below:

1. ♠ A 9 7 6
   ♥ Q J 8 6 5 4
   ♦ Q 9
   ♣ 10

2. ♠ J 8 6 5 4 3
   ♥ A K J 8
   ♦ K 2
   ♣ 5

3. ♠ A K J 9 8
   ♥ K Q 9 3
   ♦ 9
   ♣ 10 8 7

ANSWERS

1. You have 6-4 in the majors but with reasonable hearts. I recommend just parking it in 4♥ (most would do so with a Texas transfer bid of 4♦).
2. This time you have a weak 6-card major so it is worth bidding Stayman with. If partner bids a major you can issue a slam try (do you have a way to show shortness in clubs + a fit?). If partner bids 2♦, your hand is substantially weaker and it seems best to bid 4♥, 'delayed Texas transfer' to park it in 4♠.

3. You have the 'normal' Smolen shape, 5-4 in the majors. If partner bids a major over Stayman, you can make a slam try (again, a splinter would be best). If partner does not have a major, your hand is not worth any slam try. Bid 3♥, your 4-card major, playing either 3NT or 4♠ depending on whether or not opener has a fit for spades.

Opener shows a good 4♥ raise

Suppose the bidding starts this way:

1NT	2♣
2♦	3♠

If opener has 3 hearts then he might wish to tell responder "I have a really nice hand if you are thinking about slam", versus just an ordinary hand with 3 hearts. Note that if opener always just bids 4♥ then responder has no room to cuebid and must guess whether to pass or bid RKC.

The solution is that a 4♣ rebid is artificial and says "I have slam-suitable heart raise". To me that means a maximum with reasonable values, or a 16 count with great values. On the above auction

♠ A 2
♥ A Q 3
♦ A Q 10 7 6
♣ 9 5 4

would qualify for a 4♣ bid showing a good 4♥ bid.

What should responder do over this 4♣ 'strong raise' bid? *Responder should always bid 4♦ as a RETRANSFER back to 4♥.* Opener must accept by bidding 4♥ and now opener is declarer in a heart contract. Then responder either passes or moves toward slam (normally by bidding RKC).

♠ A 2	♠ K J 8 3
♥ A Q 3	♥ K 10 7 6 5
♦ A Q 10 7 6	♦ K 2
♣ 9 5 4	♣ A 3

1NT	2♣
2♦	3♠
4♣	4♦
4♥	4NT
5♣	6♥

Responder has just enough to bid RKC once he knows opener has a strong raise. He transfers back to 4♥ by bidding 4♦ 'retransfer', then continues with RKC. If you play Kickback, then 4♠ would be RKC. Opener shows all the keycards but responder has no interest in 7 so he just signs off in 6♥.

If opener had bid 4♥ responder would have to Pass with the above hand. Imagine that instead opener had this hand:

♠ A Q 2
♥ J 4 3
♦ Q 5
♣ K Q J 8 7

Even 4♥ might go down on a bad day but you certainly don't want to get higher than that.

Opener rebids 3NT
and responder wants to try for slam

If responder has 16-17 HCP and 5-4, he can raise to 4NT, a quantitative raise. Of course he might have a good 15; with a good 17 he might drive to slam.

♠ 9 7 6	♠ A Q 5 4
♥ J 2	♥ A Q 9 5 4
♦ A K Q 8	♦ 7 4
♣ K Q 7 6	♣ A 2

1NT	2♣
2♦	3♠
3NT	4NT

Opener has an easy pass. 4NT is not 100% to make but pretty close. 6NT will make sometimes but it is against the odds.

What if responder has 6-4 and a slam try? One approach is to play that continuing over 3NT with a bid of 4♣ or 4♦ shows 6-4 in the majors and a slam try. Some like that responder is showing shortness in the bid minor; you might prefer the simpler approach of 4♣ or 4♦ just being a cuebid (I don't care personally, I think the 'cuebid' approach is fine).

Opener will look at his values but especially in the majors in judging whether or not to cooperate in a slam venture.

♠ K 8	♠ A Q 9 7 6 5
♥ A Q 3	♥ K J 10 5
♦ A 7 6 5	♦ 8
♣ Q 7 6 5	♣ A 2

1NT	2♣
2♦	3♥
3NT	4♣
4♦	4NT
5♣	6♠

Opener has a minimum but 4 great cards, and the ♣Q is not necessarily worthless (imagine responder lacked the ♥J for example). Responder is not greedy in considering a grand slam opposite a 2-card spade fit; even if opener has the ♣K and the ♥Q (the latter being very difficult to discover anyway) a grand slam needs to be better than on a 3-2 trump break, especially considering that some won't even get to a small slam.

Responder has 6-4 in the majors but no longer has slam interest

If opener bids 3NT, responder will now wish sometimes just to play in 4 of the major. If you use '4♣ or 4♦ is a cuebid' then responder just has to bid 4 of his major and play it from his side. With 6-4 and a decent hand this is no big deal.

♠ Q 2	♠ A 9 7 6 5 4
♥ K J 3	♥ A Q 9 4
♦ A J 10 8 7	♦ K 2
♣ A 8 7	♣ 9

1NT	2♣
2♦	3♥
3NT	4♠

With such a weak suit responder should give up on slam and sign off in 4♠. 3NT might sometimes be better but often, as here, opener is just denying a spade fit and isn't necessarily that enthused about playing in notrump.

Some advanced continuations

You can well skip this section unless you want to go into the nth degree on Smolen. The first question would be "what if responder is 5440? Might we not have a big fit in the 4-card minor?" Yes, though this not common. The question is what adjustments in the system are necessary to show this. We can try:

1NT	2♣
2♦	3♠
3NT	4♣: all 6-4 slam tries. This has the advantage of allowing opener to bid 4♦ 'Last Train' (another Topic article covered in Book 1)
	4♦: 5440 with 4 diamonds. Opener to place the contract
	4♥: to play
	4♠: 5440 with 4 CLUBS. This is a 'substitute bid'. Opener to place the contract. Note that this is a bid of 4 of the OTHER major (4 of responder's major is to play)
	4NT: quantitative raise

♠ K 3	♠ A Q 8 7
♥ K 2	♥ A J 10 7 6
♦ A Q 9 8	♦ K J 7 6
♣ A 7 6 5 3	♣ –

1NT	2♣
2♦	3♠
3NT	4♦
6♦	

4♦ showed 5440 with 4 diamonds and opener has an easy 6♦ bid. Getting to 7 if we belong there is almost impossible so I won't worry about superscience continuations.

The second unlikely possibility is a very strong 6-4 that has a void and wants to bid Exclusion RKC. This can be accomplished by jumping to 5 of the void over 3NT:

♠ K 2	♠ A Q 9 8 7 6
♥ A 4 3	♥ K Q J 2
♦ A K J 9	♦ –
♣ 10 7 6 3	♣ K Q J

1NT	2♣
2♦	3♥
3NT	5♦
5NT	6NT

The jump to 5♦ is 'Exclusion RKC', showing a diamond void and asking for keycards in spades, the long suit. Opener bids 5NT, the 3rd step, to show 2 keycards without the trump queen. The ♦A is excluded since responder is void. At this point it looks like 6NT might have some have play if spades don't split and since a keycard is missing opener should have good enough diamonds to play 6NT.

FINAL QUIZ

How should these pair of hands be bid?

1.	♠ K 3 2	♠ Q 10 8 7 6
	♥ Q 8 3	♥ K J 10 4
	♦ A K 7 3	♦ 2
	♣ A 8 2	♣ K 9 4

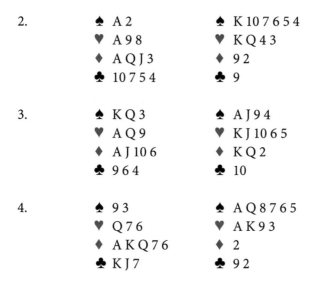

2.   ♠ A 2   ♠ K 10 7 6 5 4
           ♥ A 9 8   ♥ K Q 4 3
           ♦ A Q J 3   ♦ 9 2
           ♣ 10 7 5 4   ♣ 9

3.   ♠ K Q 3   ♠ A J 9 4
           ♥ A Q 9   ♥ K J 10 6 5
           ♦ A J 10 6   ♦ K Q 2
           ♣ 9 6 4   ♣ 10

4.   ♠ 9 3   ♠ A Q 8 7 6 5
           ♥ Q 7 6   ♥ A K 9 3
           ♦ A K Q 7 6   ♦ 2
           ♣ K J 7   ♣ 9 2

Suppose you play the advanced methods. How would this pair of hands be bid?

5.   ♠ K 2   ♠ A Q 10 8 7
           ♥ Q 9 3   ♥ A J 8 7
           ♦ K 9 3   ♦ Q J 8 4
           ♣ A Q J 8 7   ♣ –

ANSWERS

1.   1NT   2♣
           2♦   3♥
           3♠   4♠

Over 2♦, responder jumps to 3♥ to show 5 spades + 4 hearts and game forcing. Opener has a fit so he bids 3♠. Responder has room to offer 3NT or cuebid but with no interest in anything but 4♠, he signs off.

2.	1NT	2♣
	2♦	4♥
	4♠	

Responder bids Stayman, holding a weak long major and strong 4-card major. Over 2♦, responder wants to sign off in 4♠ but must do so with a 'delayed Texas transfer' of 4♥. It is advantageous on this hand to have opener play it.

3.	1NT	2♣
	2♦	3♠
	4♣	4♦
	4♥	4NT
	5♠	6♥

Opener bids 4♣ over 3♠ Smolen to show 3-card heart support and a good hand for slam. Responder bids 4♦ to retransfer back to 4♥ then bids RKC into the cold slam. The hands happen to fit well but even if opener's minors were reversed slam still has reasonable play.

4.	1NT	2♣
	2♦	3♥
	3NT	4♦
	4♠	

Opener bids 3NT over 3♥, showing a doubleton spade. Responder continues with 4♦, showing a diamond control (and no club control) and slam interest. With a terrible fit and all the wrong stuff, opener signs off in 4♠.

5.	1NT	2♣
	2♦	3♥
	3NT	4♦
	4NT	

Responder shows 5-4-4-0 with slam interest by continuing with a natural 4♦ (this requires agreeing that all 6-4 slam tries continue over 3NT by bidding 4♣). Opener has long strong clubs so he signs off in 4NT. He might try 4♠ on the 5-2 if he had weaker clubs.

Conclusion

This is all I can think of to say about Smolen. I think it is a worthwhile convention to play even if you don't adopt some of the 'bells and whistles' that I offer here. Enjoy!

6
Developments after a strong 2♣ opening

Opening 2♣ with a strong balanced hand

The strong 2♣ opening is the cornerstone of strong hand bidding in most modern systems. In the original systems strong 2-bids were used which made big hand bidding easier, but at the loss of the more-useful preempts that are used in the current era.

The first question is "what hands qualify for a strong 2♣ opening?". If your hand is relatively balanced, then the normal approach is this:

- opening 2NT = 20–21 HCP;
- opening 2♣ with a flat hand shows 22+ HCP.

A hand with 22–23 HCP would normally plan to rebid 2NT, which is strongly invitational but not quite forcing. With 24+ and a balanced hand, opener will want to force to game.

In standard methods, a response of 2♦ to the 2♣ opening is artificial and 'waiting', i.e. saying nothing specific. This is to allow the big hand, opener, maximum space to describe his hand. This would be the development of balanced hands:

OPENER	RESPONDER
2♣	2♦

- 2NT: 22–23
- 3NT: 24 or more ('24+')

Bidding after a 2NT rebid follows this rule: *use the same systems that you would use had the opening been 2NT.*
Example:

OPENER	RESPONDER
♠ K Q 8 3	♠ J 6 5 4
♥ A 2	♥ 8 3
♦ A K Q 3	♦ J 4 2
♣ A 10 3	♣ Q 9 4 2
2♣	2♦
2NT	3♣
3♠	4♠

Opener, with 22 balanced HCP, has a minimum 2♣ opening with such a flat hand. Responder bids 2♦ waiting. 2NT shows 22-23 balanced. Now 'system on' applies, and 3♣ is Stayman and the 4-4 spade fit is reached. Not that 4♠ will always make but it is by far the best contract.

Of course, there are a number of possible alternatives, such as Puppet Stayman if you play that.

If opener rebids 3NT, I still suggest using Stayman and transfers but now it has to be, inconveniently, at the 4-level. If responder has a weak 5-card major, then he has to guess and he would normally pass 3NT for better or worse.

OPENER	RESPONDER
♠ A 2	♠ J 8 6 5 4
♥ K Q 10 3	♥ J
♦ A K Q	♦ J 10 8 7
♣ A Q 10 3	♣ J 9 2

2♣	2♦
3NT	Pass?

Responder lacks the space to investigate a spade fit and passes, hoping that opener can make at least 9 tricks even if there is a spade fit and 3NT is much better than 4♠ here. Try switching opener's spades and hearts and then 3NT will be down on a heart lead and 4♠ will make easily.

This problem is solved by some using a 2-way 2♥ rebid. In the USA this convention is called 'Kokish'.

Opening 2♣ with a long major

My theory is that you open 2♣ on good playing hands that need significantly less than the values required for a response to a 1 major opening for game. Thus fairly strong hands that are relatively balanced do not qualify for 2♣. Examples:

OPENER 1	OPENER 2
♠ A K 9 4 3	♠ K Q
♥ K 4	♥ A Q 8 6 5
♦ A K J 3	♦ A Q
♣ Q 3	♣ A 9 5 4

Opener 1 has 20 HCP but is not close to a 2♣ opening; you need the values of a response to make a game, either a raise or 5/6 HCP with no fit.

Opener 2 has 21 HCP but with weak long suits the hand still needs 'response values' for game and should open 1♥.

I think that with 21 HCP and a 5-card major, I do try to open 2♣ but if I am 5422 I need a well-constructed hand. I would open 2♣ with either of these hands:

OPENER 3	OPENER 4
♠ A K J 10 3	♠ K Q 10
♥ A K 10 4	♥ A Q J 9 7
♦ A Q	♦ 3
♣ 9 4	♣ A K Q 8

Opener 3 is 5422 so needs to be 'well constructed' which with good spots and combined diamond honors seems to qualify to me. Imagine partner with ♠ 9xx ♥ Qxx ♦ xxx ♣ xxxx and you have a play for 4♠.

Opener 4 is 5431 with a small singleton and good suits. I think it is easier to open 2♣ and hope that partner is not completely broke than open a very wide-range 1♥ and hope to guess what to do later.

With 22+ HCP and a major I would always open 2♣; if the hand is 5332 I would likely plan a notrump rebid; with 5422 this is also possible in rare cases with strong doubletons.

I also like to open 2♣ with a long major and 17-20 HCP if the playing strength is strong. With 17 HCP I would have either a strong 7+ card major or a 6-5+ 2-suiter. Of course the high cards need to be working. More examples:

OPENER 5	OPENER 6
♠ A K Q 10 7 6 5	♠ –
♥ A K J	♥ A K J 9 8 7
♦ 2	♦ A 3
♣ 9 7	♣ K Q 10 8 7

Opener 5 almost has 'game in hand' if the spades are solid and the ♥J takes a trick.

♠ xxx ♥ xx ♦ xxxx ♣ xxxx would almost always be enough to make 4♠.

Opener 6 needs very little for game, probably just xxx in hearts or the ♣J. There are two more reasons to open these hands 2♣:

1. it makes slam bidding easier when you show your strong potential immediately, and
2. you are less likely to get competitive bidding when you open at a higher level (2♣) and if you do you have at least created a 'forcing situation' where you have to either reach game or double the opponents.

As the hand gets stronger in HCP, it can be a bit weaker in playing strength but still needs to have prospects of 10 tricks in the major opposite not much. Two more examples:

OPENER 7	OPENER 8
♠ A K Q 10 6 5	♠ A K J 8
♥ A K 3	♥ A K Q J 9 3
♦ K 10 9	♦ –
♣ 8	♣ 10 8 3

It was once said "you can always play partner for the right queen", which means that if all you need for game is a particular queen, you are entitled to make that assumption. In many cases partner has more than that and rarely has less.

With opener 7 game will have good play opposite either red queen.

Opener 8 will make opposite the ♠Q and might make opposite no queen.

This is just my opinion and from what I see, not mainstream practice; most open these hands with 1 of a major. In any event, it is good to discuss with partner where you draw the line for opening 2♣.

Opening 2♣ with a long minor

Now you must have either 22+ HCP (and not always in that case), or strong prospects for 3NT or 11+ tricks in your long minor. Examples:

Opener 1	Opener 2	Opener 3
♠ A K Q 2	♠ A 5	♠ –
♥ 3	♥ A 10 3	♥ A 3
♦ A K 8 7 6	♦ A K Q J 8 7 6	♦ A K J 9 3
♣ A J 4	♣ 3	♣ K Q J 10 8 7

Opener 1 I would open 1♦. I have 21 HCP and a small singleton but with the long suit a minor I would open 1♦. This makes it easier to find a 4-4 spade fit and of course we might want to play it in 1♦.

Opener 2 should open 2♣ since you have 3NT in hand if they don't cash 5 fast club tricks.

Opener 3 should also open 2♣ since you need virtually nothing to make 5 of a minor.

If you are 4441, you have a real problem. If you have something like stiff king, most treat the hand as balanced and with 22+ would open 2♣ and rebid in notrump. With a different singleton, try to open 1 of a minor since there is no descriptive rebid after starting with 2♣. I would say with 23+ HCP you must open 2♣ however.

Responses to a 2♣ opening

The simplest method is '2♦ waiting'. The 2♦ response doesn't show or deny much in particular, you are just leaving opener maximum room to show his hand.

Some hands do call for an immediate positive response in a suit. The standard I most often hear is 'at least 2 of the top 3 honors in the suit'. This means that with KQ432 and nothing else you can make a positive, and with AJ10987 and a side ace you have to wait with 2♦. This makes no sense to me.

I say that you should respond 2 of a major with a good 5, or reasonable 6+ card suit and a hand that has strong slam prospects opposite a fit. This is especially true when responder has hearts since that suit can be bid cheaply. Examples:

Responder 1	Responder 2	Responder 3
♠ K Q 8 7 6	♠ 9	♠ K 10 8 6 5
♥ 9 2	♥ K J 9 6 5 4	♥ A
♦ J 8 7 6	♦ A 2	♦ Q J 9 3
♣ 8 3	♣ J 10 8 7	♣ 9 7 6

Responder 1 should bid 2♦ in my opinion. You are not strong enough to expect an easy slam opposite say 22 balanced HCP and 3 spades. If partner rebids 2NT you can transfer and get it played from the correct side, thinking about slam if opener can super-accept (show a good 4-card raise).

Responder 2 should bid 2♥. You don't have KQ+ in hearts but with a 6-card suit this should not be a requirement. You have a lot to say so best to start saying it. Note that you want to be relaxed about requirements for a 2♥ response because it does not preempt opener from showing any other long suit.

Responder 3 has plenty of values for a 2♠ response but I prefer 2♦. If opener has long hearts it will be so much better to let him bid hearts; then you can bid spades and see what develops. With the ♥A in the spade suit, I would respond 2♠ to emphasize the slam-mish and spade orientation of the hand, in spite of the preemption should opener have hearts.

Responding 2NT

If this is used as a natural bid, it should show at least 9 HCP and spread-around values (to make notrump from that side practical). It can actually be a useful convention if it promises a 4333 shape and at least 3 controls.

OPENER	RESPONDER
♠ A K 9 8 7 6	♠ Q 10 3
♥ 2	♥ A 8 7
♦ A Q 10 3	♦ K 9 4 2
♣ A K	♣ 8 7 6

2♣	2NT
3♠	4♦
4NT	5♦
5♥	6♦
7♠	

2NT shows 4333 with spread out values and at least 3 controls. 4♦ is a control bid (a spade fit is known when responder has 4333). The rest is Roman Keycard Blackwood (RKC); adjust the responses according to your preferred methods. 6♦ shows the ♦K and the ♠Q, but no other kings.

Of course it is possible to get to 7 by responding 2♦ but this is a smoother way.

Over 2NT, a 3♣ bid by opener should ask for the 4-card suit. If responder has a major he bids it, with diamonds he bids 3♦. With 4 clubs, he bids 3NT (or possibly 4♣ with a better hand, say 11+).

OPENER	RESPONDER
♠ A K Q 3	♠ J 10 8 7
♥ A	♥ Q 9 3
♦ K Q J 8 7	♦ A 9 4
♣ A 10 3	♣ K 8 4

2♣	2NT
3♣	3♠
4NT	5♦
5NT	6♣
7♠	

3♣ is 'Stayman' for the 4-card suit which responder shows naturally. RKC takes care of the rest. One advantage of the 2NT response is that opener, who usually has shape, can take over and not leave it to responder to bid RKC later with all his extra HCP and have no idea whether to bid 7 or not.

Responding 3 of a minor

These responses are so preemptive that I think they should be confined to one-suited hands. A 6-card suit would be normal, with a good suit. KJ10xxx and a side king would be the worst hand. KQJxx and a side king would be a minimum if 5332.

Even so, responder is left with no good bid if opener bids 3 of a major and responder can't raise.

OPENER	RESPONDER
2♣	3♦
3♥	?

If responder has ♠xxx ♥xx ♦KQJxx ♣Kxx, now what?

Responder can bid 3♠, known not to be a suit if you agree that the 3♦ response shows a one-suited hand, as a waiting bid.

You could raise hearts but with xx I think that is misleading. Opener can rebid hearts if he wants to.

With a particularly good suit, say KQJ10xx, responder can ignore a side suit of say Jxxx and bid 3 of his long minor anyway.

Responses of 3♥ or 3♠

These typically show KQJ10xx in the major, i.e. a semi-solid suit.

Higher level responses would occur rarely and would have to be the subject of another topic.

Other popular responding systems to a 2♣ opening

The most popular alternative in the USA is '2♥ double negative'. A 2♦ response is waiting but is forcing to game. With a really poor hand the response is 2♥, also artificial and waiting.

The exact standards for a 2♥ response vary. A couple you might consider:

- respond 2♦ when holding at least an ace, king, or two queens;
- respond 2♥ on any hand with no controls (A or K).

The advantage of this method is that a 2♦ response is game forcing, which removes the need for a 'second negative' that is commonly played when using 2♦ waiting:

Opener	Responder
2♣	2♦
2♥	3♣: artificial, 2nd negative

The term 'second negative' is a bit misleading because 2♦ waiting is not a 'first negative' but a neutral waiting bid. That is, unless you play mandatory responses of 2♥ and higher with positive hands. In any event, if a 2♥ response is 'double negative' then when you respond 2♦, game forcing, the 3♣ bid in the above auction should be used as natural.

There are two drawbacks to '2♥ double negative':

1. *Opener is preempted when he has long hearts.* This is obvious – if responder has bid 2♥ then opener can't bid 2♥ himself.
2. *Responder can't bid 2♥ as a natural positive response.* Most play that a 2NT response shows a positive response in

hearts, but this is more preemptive and could wrongside notrump.

Still, there are advantages to knowing that responder has something when he responds 2♦.

Getting out below game after a 2♣ opening

This doesn't happen often, normally when it does it is a 2NT rebid that is passed. This is why a 2♣ opening should show close to game forcing values. If a 2♦ response is waiting and opener bids a suit that is of course forcing. I would say that a 3 of a minor rebid should be forcing to game. A rebid of 2 of a major could lead to a partial if responder follows with a bid of 3♣ to confirm a weak hand (called 'second negative'):

OPENER	RESPONDER
2♣	2♦
2♠	3♣: 2nd negative

It is important to know what sequences could be played under game after this start. First of all, responder must bid 3♣ second negative; other bids are forcing to game. Second of all, over 3♣, opener's new suit rebids are forcing. Only if he rebids his major can responder pass below game.

OPENER	RESPONDER
♠ A K J 10 7 6	♠ 2
♥ A K 3	♥ J 8 7 6
♦ A Q 3	♦ 9 7 6 5 4
♣ 8	♣ 10 7 6
2♣	2♦
2♠	3♣: 2nd negative
3♠	Pass

Keep in mind that responder should pass 3♠ only with a truly terrible hand. Opener thinks he can make game opposite the right queen so if responder has a queen, he may as well assume it is the right queen and take it to game in most cases.

What if opener rebids a new suit and responder then returns to opener's major at the 3-level? This is a debatable point but I would say this should not be forcing. If responder has any values at all he should bid game. I would say that if he raises the second suit that should be forcing. All opener needs on many of these deals is a fit in one of his suits.

OPENER	RESPONDER	
2♣	2♦	
2♠	3♣	
3♦	3♠:	can be passed
	4♦:	should not be passed

If the response is 2♥ 'double negative', the same questions can arise. I suggest:

- opener's new suit is forcing;
- responder's raises are forcing.

So, if opener bids and rebids his suit responder can pass. Or, if opener bids a new suit and responder takes simple preference back to opener's first suit, he can pass. This is similar to the 'second negative' auctions we just discussed.

OPENER	RESPONDER	
2♣	2♥:	double negative
3♦	3♥	
4♦:	responder can pass	

Control showing responses to a 2♣ opening

Some favor showing responder's number of controls (A = 2 controls, K = 1 control). It can work like this:

OPENER	RESPONDER	
2♣	2♦:	0 or 1 control
	2♥:	2 controls
	2♠:	3 controls
	2NT:	4 or more controls

3 of a suit responses would show semisolid 6+ card suits and not specify the controls. I have seen others distinguish between 0 and 1 control, and between 3 controls that are in the same suit (AK) or spread out between at least two suits.

This can be useful if opener has a self-sufficient type of hand and can use the control information to place the contract. The rather big downside is that the auction is considerably preempted if there is a need for an exchange of natural bids. This was popular back when I started playing but I don't see many expert partnerships using it these days.

Game or higher sequences after a 2♦ response

There are some questions to consider. For example:

OPENER	RESPONDER
2♣	2♦
2♠	4♠

What should this jump raise show, as opposed to raising to 3♠? I like what is called 'Fast Arrival' in general – jumping to game is a discouraging bid (in a game forcing auction), while raising under game shows a better hand. You might want to keep it simple and stick with that. If so then a raise to 3♠ in the above auction should show at least a useful looking 5 or 6 points. For example, having the queen of trump and a side king should justify a 3♠ raise.

If you are using '3♣ second negative', then you might agree that with weaker raises you start with 3♣, then put partner in game next round. A jump raise can be more of a 'picture bid' showing at least 4 trump but no side suit controls (A, K, or singleton/void).

I think this idea is close, but I prefer that the jump to 4 of the major show the A or K of trumps, at least 4 card support, but no other side controls. This is a hand that is more likely to produce a slam and is hard to express otherwise. If you really want to get fancy, opener can bid a new suit to ask for third round control of that suit:

OPENER	RESPONDER
♠ A J 10 8 7 6	♠ K 9 4 3
♥ A K J 3	♥ 8 2
♦ A K Q	♦ 9 7 6 5
♣ –	♣ J 10 3

2♣	2♦
2♠	4♠
5♥	6♠
7♠	

After the 'picture' 4♠ raise, opener assumes the queen will drop and the trumps are solid. He bids 5♥ to ask for third round control of hearts and when he hears 6♠ to confirm that control he bids the grand. Even if trump are 3-0 you have play if you guess which hand has the 3 trump.

What should happen after the raise to 3 of the major? You could simply say that opener should cuebid his lowest control and cuebid up-the-line as you would in normal auctions:

OPENER	RESPONDER
2♣	2♦
2♠	3♠
4♦: denies a club control	

Not many 2♣ openings have an uncontrolled suit however, but they often contain length in a side suit. Many experts in the US play that opener's new suit is a side suit (maybe only 3 cards). Responder should look at his holding in that suit when making a close decision:

OPENER	RESPONDER
♠ A K 10 8 7	♠ Q 9 3
♥ A Q 8 7 6	♥ K 9 3
♦ A K	♦ J 8 7 6
♣ 2	♣ J 6 5

2♣	2♦
2♠	3♠
4♥	5♥
5♠	6♠

4♥ shows side length so responder bids 5♥ to show a useful heart holding. Opener has a hole in trump and is missing an ace so he bids a non-forcing 5♠. Responder raises holding the trump queen. With a fourth heart responder would try 6♥ to suggest playing the slam in hearts if opener so chooses.

Other auctions that don't involve a direct raise are natural (or include 3♣ 'second negative'). Responder can wait with 2NT over 2 of a major if no other bid fits.

OPENER	RESPONDER
2♣	2♦
2♥	2NT

2NT is a general purpose waiting bid to give opener more room to show what he has. Responder's new suit bids show at least a 5-card suit. Thus the 2NT bid denies 5 spades but might include 4 spades so opener needs to look for that fit if he has 4 spades himself.

If 3♣ is a second negative, then the 2NT bid might have to be made with a club suit and reasonable values, which by the way I would say is at least 4-5 HCP; with less I would bid 3♣ second negative planning to bid game next time unless I really have nothing. Do not bid 3♣ second negative if you hold an ace.

Opener rebids 3 of a minor

This is an awkward auction to be sure, which is why many good hands with a minor are opened 1 of a minor instead of 2♣. If opener rebids 3♣, I advise that a 3♦ reply be waiting (rather than second negative per se). This gives opener room to bid a 4-card major or 3NT if he wishes.

OPENER	RESPONDER
♠ A K J 3	♠ 10 8 6 5
♥ A Q 3	♥ K 9 4
♦ 2	♦ J 7 6 5
♣ A K Q 8 7	♣ 10 3

2♣	2♦
3♣	3♦
3♠	4♠

3♦ is waiting over 3♣, and the raise is weak. Opener has shown a very good hand to open 2♣ then bid a minor so responder needs to be aggressive with a fit. Opener trustingly passes 4♠.

If opener rebids 3♦, responder's bid of 3 of a major should show a 5+-card suit. Thus, responder has to close his eyes and bid 3NT with some number of hands he is not thrilled about.

Opener's jump rebid can set trump and demand cuebidding. Responder bids his cheapest ace. Lacking this he bids 3NT to show at least one king, opener can then either ask for the king, or bid the cheapest side suit where a king would be useful.

OPENER	RESPONDER
♠ A K Q J 10 7 6 5	♠ 2
♥ A Q J 3	♥ K 9 4
♦ 2	♦ Q 8 7 6 5 4
♣ –	♣ Q 8 7

2♣	2♦
3♠	3NT
4♥	5♥
6♠	

3♠ set trump. 3NT showed at least one king but no aces. 4♥ was the cheapest side suit where a king would be useful. 5♥ shows the ♥K.

Summary and conclusion

Clearly there was a lot more we could have said about 2♣ openings but that was all there was room for in this chapter.

Good luck and enjoy!

7
Lebensohl

Introduction and abbreviations

Lebensohl refers to a 2NT bid, in certain auctions, that requests that partner bid 3♣. Such a convention has been referred to as a 'Puppet', i.e. partner is instructed to do something (make the cheapest available bid) but not showing anything specific. This is different from a Jacoby transfer bid of 2♦, that also requests the cheap bid (2♥) but promises a heart suit.

Like many conventions, it had a limited original application and over time players have found additional uses for it.

The following abbreviations will be used:

LHO	=	Left Hand Opponent
RHO	=	Right Hand Opponent
INV	=	Invitational
INV+	=	Invitational or better
GF	=	Game Forcing
HCP	=	High Card Points
RKC	=	Roman Keycard Blackwood
LEB	=	Lebensohl

2NT Lebensohl after partner opens 1NT

Suppose you are responder in this auction, with opponents' bids shown in brackets:

	1NT*	(2♠)	?
*15–17 HCP			

1.
- ♠ 3
- ♥ A Q 7 5 4
- ♦ K J 3 2
- ♣ 10 7 6

2.
- ♠ J 7
- ♥ Q J 9 7 6 5
- ♦ Q 2
- ♣ 8 5 4

With hand 1 you want to bid 3♥ but you want it to be forcing. If 3♥ was forcing it would show five hearts and ask opener to raise with three-card support. With only two hearts hopefully opener has a spade stopper to bid 3NT with.

With hand 2 you want to bid 3♥ to play in 3♥. Of course a 3♥ bid can't have both meanings, so the Lebensohl 2NT convention was devised for the weaker type (2). Opener puppets to 3♣, then when you next bid 3♥, he knows you want to play it in 3♥. Bidding 3♥ directly is forcing (1).

1.	1NT	(2♠)	3♥:	forcing.
2.	1NT	(2♠)	2NT:	Lebensohl, forces 3♣.

Now 3♥ by responder: to play in 3♥.

In it's simplest form:

- bidding directly at the three-level is forcing to game;
- bidding 2NT then a new suit that is *lower ranking* than the overcalled suit is to play.

1NT	(2♠)	2NT	(Pass)
3♣	(Pass)	?	

- Pass: the way to play in 3♣
- 3♦: to play in 3♦
- 3♥: to play in 3♥

As you can see there are some unused followup bids:

- 3NT;
- a cuebid (bid in the opponent's suit);
- a bid of a higher-ranking suit.

Suppose partner opens 1NT (15-17 HCP unless otherwise noted) and RHO overcalls 2♠. What would you want to bid with the hands below?

1.
    ♠ 7 6
    ♥ K 8 3
    ♦ A Q J 3
    ♣ Q 10 4 3

2.
    ♠ K 6
    ♥ 8 5 4
    ♦ A Q J 3
    ♣ Q 10 4 3

With hand 1 you want to bid 3NT but want to play there only if opener has a spade stopper. With hand 2 you want to play 3NT regardless. Playing 'LEB' (Lebensohl 2NT), you can bid 3NT directly or by bidding 2NT first. Bidding 2NT first is called getting there 'slow', bidding directly is 'fast':

1NT	(2♠)	3NT: fast	

1NT	(2♠)	2NT	(Pass)
3♣	(Pass)	3NT: slow	

We know that one sequence should show a spade stopper and the other deny a stopper. There isn't a lot to decide which way to play, whichever you will remember is better. Most play 'fast denies' or 'slow shows' (a stopper), two ways of saying the same thing. If this is your agreement, the direct 3NT denies a stopper and 2NT then 3NT shows a stopper.

If you want to cuebid their suit for Stayman, then you should use the same 'fast' and 'slow' rules that you used for 3NT. Playing 'fast denies':

1NT	(2♠)	3♠: four hearts, game forcing, but no spade stopper

1NT	(2♠)	2NT	(Pass)
3♣	(Pass)	3♠: four hearts, game forcing, has a spade stopper	

QUIZ 1

Time for a quiz. You are playing 'fast denies'.

| 1NT | (2♥) | what is your plan? |

1. ♠ K 3 2
   ♥ 2
   ♦ A Q 10 8 7 6
   ♣ A 4 3

2. ♠ K 8 6
   ♥ A 2
   ♦ K Q 9 3
   ♣ 10 8 6 5

3. ♠ A J 8 6
   ♥ 8 6
   ♦ J 9 8
   ♣ K Q 10 7

4. ♠ J 8 7
   ♥ 8 7
   ♦ J 2
   ♣ K J 10 8 7 6

ANSWERS

1. Bid 3♦, game forcing. You might belong in 5♦ or 6♦. In any event you don't want to play 3NT if opener lacks a heart stopper.
2. 2NT, planning to bid 3NT, 'slow with stopper'.
3. 3♥, 'fast denies' stopper. Since you cuebid, you show four cards in the other major.
4. 2NT, forcing 3♣, planning to pass.

Using Lebensohl with a higher ranking suit

If you have a higher ranking suit than the overcall, you can bid your suit at the two-level with a competitive hand. If you go to the three-level voluntarily, you must show either an invitational hand or a game forcing hand.

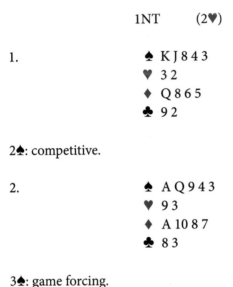

1NT   (2♥)

1.   ♠ K J 8 4 3
            ♥ 3 2
            ♦ Q 8 6 5
            ♣ 9 2

2♠: competitive.

2.   ♠ A Q 9 4 3
            ♥ 9 3
            ♦ A 10 8 7
            ♣ 8 3

3♠: game forcing.

3.   ♠ A J 10 4 3
            ♥ 2
            ♦ K 8 4 3
            ♣ 9 4 3

2NT: Lebensohl, then (over opener's 3♣) 3♠: invitational.

Finishing GF sequences

If responder has shown a stopper ('slow with stopper') then opener's task is simple:

1NT	(2♥)	2NT	(Pass)
3♣	(Pass)	3NT: 'slow with stopper'; this is an absolute sign-off	

1NT	(2♥)	2NT	(Pass)
3♣	(Pass)	3♥: Stayman with stopper, i.e. has four spades also	

Opener has only two choices: bid spades with 4+ spades, or bid 3NT. If responder denies a stopper, then opener knows to avoid 3NT if he lacks one also. Look at these two hands:

♠ 9 4 3	♠ J 2
♥ K Q 3	♥ A 8 2
♦ K Q J 5 2	♦ A 10 4 3
♣ K J	♣ 10 8 6 5

1NT	(2♠)	3NT [no stopper]	(Pass)
4♦	= natural, no spade stopper		

As you can see you have no play at all for any game but will make 4♦ if you lose only one club trick.

So, *opener's removal to four of a minor can be passed.*

If responder had a better hand, say

♠ 8 2
♥ A 8 2
♦ A 10 4 3
♣ A 10 9 3

he would raise and have hope of making 5♦.

The auction could be similar if responder shows a 'no stopper Stayman' hand with a 'fast denies' direct cuebid.

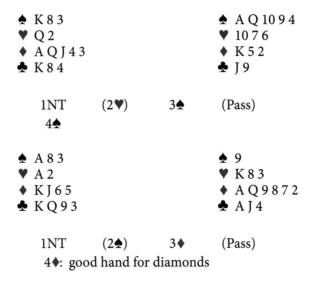

```
♠ 9 3            ♠ 8 2
♥ K Q 9          ♥ A J 8 4
♦ A K 4 3        ♦ Q J 2
♣ A 8 6 5        ♣ K 9 4 3

     1NT     (2♠)      3♠      (Pass)
             [four hearts, no stopper]
     4♥: try the 4-3 fit!
```

Of course 4♥ doesn't have to work but it seems as good a shot as any.

If responder bids a new suit, GF, at the three-level, he is seeking a raise with a suitable hand. If the suit is a major, then 3+ card support will do. If the suit is a minor, opener needs some trick-taking potential for the minor to bypass 3NT.

```
♠ K 8 3          ♠ A Q 10 9 4
♥ Q 2            ♥ 10 7 6
♦ A Q J 4 3      ♦ K 5 2
♣ K 8 4          ♣ J 9

     1NT     (2♥)      3♠      (Pass)
     4♠
```

```
♠ A 8 3          ♠ 9
♥ A 2            ♥ K 8 3
♦ K J 6 5        ♦ A Q 9 8 7 2
♣ K Q 9 3        ♣ A J 4

     1NT     (2♠)      3♦      (Pass)
     4♦: good hand for diamonds
```

Responder will keycard into 6♦. It is very tough to get to seven if responder is in control of the auction. Opener might bid seven if he bids RKC himself, as he has the trick source in clubs. This would be more clear with KQJx or KQ10xx in clubs.

If opener can't raise and doesn't have a stopper, he cuebids the opponent's suit at the three-level, if possible; after

1NT   (2♠)   3♥   (Pass)

bid 3♠ with:

♠ J 8 7
♥ K 2
♦ A K J 8
♣ K 10 7 6.

If responder doesn't bid 3NT you will hopefully land in a playable fit, perhaps 4♥ on a 5-2 fit. The problem is acute when there is no room to cuebid at the three-level; after

1NT   (2♥)   3♠   (Pass)

you have no obvious bid with:

♠ J 3
♥ 10 4 3
♦ A K J 10 3
♣ A Q 3

Whatever you do you will guess wrong sometimes. I recommend bidding 4♦, natural, hoping that 5♦ or 4♠ are playable contracts. This brings up the point that with a hand like

♠ A 8 6 5 2
♥ K Q 2
♦ Q 2
♣ 10 7 6

responder should anticipate this problem and either place the contract in 3NT (via LEB 2NT 'slow with stopper'), or search for 5-4 spades only by bidding 2NT then 3♥.

What if opener has a good raise of responder's major? In the auction above, he bids 4♥ (since four of a minor would be natural); after

1NT   (2♥)   3♠   (Pass)

bid 4♥ with:

♠ K J 8 3
♥ A 2
♦ A K J 7
♣ 9 7 6

You have a fourth trump and well-placed assets, so show the 'strong raise' by cuebidding 4♥. I don't believe that you promise a heart control since it is your only available strong-raise bid. For example with the above hand, if the ♥A was the ♣A, you should still bid 4♥.

If opener can cuebid the opponent's suit at the three-level, then I suggest that *any bid at the four-level should be a 'good raise' cuebid:*

1NT   (2♠)   3♥   (Pass)

3♠: mandatory with only two hearts and no spade stopper
3NT: mandatory with only two hearts but has a spade stopper
4♣ or 4♦: must therefore be good heart raises

This type of 'negative inference' might be tough for some. Play it only if firmly agreed with partner.

Transfer Lebensohl

A LEB variation that has gained considerable popularity is called 'Transfer Lebensohl'. In the easiest version, any bid responder makes at the three-level is a transfer, showing *at least invitational values:*

1NT   (2♥)

2NT: LEB, as usual
3♣: INV+ with diamonds
3♦: like a 3♥ 'fast denies' cuebid
3♥: INV+ with spades (5+)
3♠: GF, long clubs

The main advantages of this approach are:

1. We get the value of a transfer bid into opener's hand, which works well if opener has something to be led around into.
2. Responder gets to show an INV hand with diamonds, not possible in 'simple LEB'.

1NT   (2♠)   3♣*   (Pass)

* INV+ with diamonds

3NT: has spade stopper and reason to accept the invitation
3♦: willing to stop in 3♦; might have only two diamonds
3♠: good hand but no spade stopper; might stop in 4♦ if responder has no stopper either and is willing to stop

Quiz 2

What would you bid, playing 'fast denies' and 'transfer LEB' in this auction? Do you have a followup plan?

1NT   (2♥)   ?

1.   ♠ A J 9 4 3
          ♥ 2
          ♦ K J 9 3
          ♣ J 10 3

2.   ♠ K 3
          ♥ 9 2
          ♦ K J 10 8 7 3
          ♣ 9 5 4

3.   ♠ K J 10 4
          ♥ 10 4
          ♦ A Q 9 3
          ♣ 10 8 7

4.   ♠ A 3 2
          ♥ 2
          ♦ K 3
          ♣ K 10 8 7 6 5 3

ANSWERS

1. Bid 3♥, a transfer showing 5+ spades and INV+ values. You have enough for game and even if opener bids 3♠ non-forcing, you plan to bid again. What you should bid then I will discuss below.

2. Bid 3♣, showing 5+ diamonds and INV+ values. If opener bids 3♦ non-forcing you will pass. If opener bids 3♥ to ask

for a stopper, you will bid 4♦ non-forcing. You are hoping
of course to hear partner bid 3NT.
3. Bid 3♦, a transfer to a cuebid of 3♥, 'fast denies', to show
   GF with four spades and no heart stopper.
4. Bid 3♠ to show a GF hand with long clubs. It makes more
   sense if you reflect that clubs transfers to diamonds, diamonds to hearts, hearts to spades, so spades must transfer
   back to clubs.

Hand 1 has a significant problem if opener bids 3♠, non-forcing. Should you continue with 3NT, hoping opener has a stopper?
One way to solve this dilemma is for opener to bid 3NT with two
spades and a stopper, even if minimum. This way, the 3♠ bid shows
either a minimum plus fit, or two spades and no stopper. This is a
bit unwieldy so you might wish to read the next section.

Modified Transfer Lebensohl

Some find the previous method, that everything at the three-level
is a transfer, easier than alternatives. Others dislike that 'a cue bid
isn't a cue bid'. There are also technical reasons. This is the modified scheme:

1NT   (2 in a major)

3♣: INV+ with diamonds
3♦: INV+ with the other major
cue bid: fast denies stopper, Stayman
three of the other major: clubs, GF

Remember the problem hand with 5-1-4-3 shape? Try it with
the modified transfer response system:

1NT   (2♥)   3♦*   (Pass)

* 5+ spades, INV+

3♥: any hand with no fit and no stopper
3♠: fit but minimum
3NT: two-card fit, stopper; might be minimum

At least you will know, should opener lack a fit, whether or not he has a heart stopper.

The opponents compete over a Lebensohl 2NT

1NT	(2♥)	2NT	(3♥)
?			

Opener can only assume for the moment that responder has a sign-off in a lower-ranking suit, clubs or diamonds. Thus opener should normally pass. If it comes back to responder:

1NT	(2♥)	2NT	(3♥)
Pass	(Pass)	?	

Pass: wanted to compete to three of a minor but not four
3♠: INV with 5+ spades, if playing 'basic LEB'. If you are playing a form of transfer LEB, then we need to agree what this means (you could play that 3♠ here shows four spades + stopper, the only logical possibility)
3NT: has heart stopper and is to play
Double: penalty
4♣ or 4♦: wants to compete, to play

If RHO bids a new suit, opener can double for penalty otherwise should pass. Responder's bids in the reopening seat follow similar lines to the above.

If RHO doubles the 2NT bid, opener should normally pass, or possibly redouble to show a maximum. Responder can bail out to his suit if he has a weak hand.

Lebensohl when the opponents overcall two of a minor

If the overcall is 2♣, many prefer to play 'system on':

1NT   (2♣)

Double: Stayman
2♦, 2♥: Jacoby
2♠: club transfer – or whatever 2♠ is directly over 1NT - (Pass)
etc.

If you don't play 'system on', then you could play 2NT as LEB but since there are no lower-ranking suits you would probably want to play 2NT as natural and invitational.

If they overcall 2♦, then 2NT should be LEB.

1NT   (2♦)

2♥, 2♠: natural, non-forcing
2NT: LEB; might be sign-off in 3♣

The three-level bids depend on whether you are using Transfer LEB. If no:

1NT   (2♦)

3♣: GF, natural
3♦: Stayman, no stopper
3♥, 3♠: GF, five-card suit

If yes:

1NT   (2♦)

3♣: Stayman, no stopper
3♦: INV+, 5+ hearts
3♥: INV+, 5+ spades
3♠: GF, clubs

♠ A K 3	♠ Q 10 8 7
♥ K 8 3	♥ A J 2
♦ 9 2	♦ 8 3
♣ K Q 9 7 6	♣ A J 10 3

1NT   (2♦)   3♣ [Stayman, no stopper]   (Pass)

4♣: natural, no major, no diamond stopper either --
5♣: should have some play.

Artificial overcalls over 1NT

There are numerous possibilities, but an artificial overcall is one
that does not promise the suit bid. There are two types: those that
do have a known suit (called an 'anchor suit'), and those that have
no known anchor suit. Examples that have an anchor suit:

> 1NT   (2♦): Astro, showing
> spades plus an
> unknown second
> suit.

> 1NT   (2♦): transfer
> overcall, showing
> hearts.

Assume the overcall was in the SHOWN suit for purposes of LEB.

1NT	(2♦):	showing spades plus an unknown second suit

3♣, 3♦, 3♥: natural, GF
3♠: no spade stopper, Stayman

Using Transfer LEB (the version where 3♦ shows 5+ in the other Major):

1NT	(2♦):	showing hearts, LEB

3♣: INV+ with diamonds
3♦: 5+ spades, INV+
3♥: no heart stopper, Stayman
3♠: GF, clubs

♠ A 2	♠ K 6 5
♥ K J 8 3	♥ A Q 9 4
♦ A K J 8	♦ Q 7 6 4
♣ 9 4 3	♣ 8 2

1NT	(2♦*)	2NT	(Pass)
3♣	(Pass)	3♠	(Pass)
4♥			

* spades + second suit

Note that the 'stopper' aspect of LEB can only refer to a suit that they are known to have, i.e. we can't talk about stoppers in the unknown second suit.

If there is no anchor suit then there should be no such thing as 'slow' and 'fast'.

<table>
<tr><td>1NT</td><td>(2♦):</td><td>overcall in either major</td></tr>
</table>

3NT: to play
2NT: LEB
three-level: standard or Transfer LEB

<table>
<tr><td>1NT</td><td>(2♦)</td></tr>
</table>

3♣: INV+, diamonds
3♦: INV+, hearts
3♥: INV+, spades
3♠: GF, clubs; note that there is no Stayman bid

I recommend that double of these artificial overcalls (not 2♣ overcalls, if you play 'system on' over that) shows points (8+ if partner shows 15-17). Once we find out what overcaller has it is easier to look for a 4-4 major suit fit or a stopper.

The overcall shows two specific suits

Can only deal with one suit.

<table>
<tr><td>1NT</td><td>(2♦):</td><td>both majors</td></tr>
</table>

3NT: to play
2NT and up: normal LEB according to agreement

Again, if you double 2♦ to show values you can then deal with stoppers.

Other uses for Lebensohl

Many have been concocted. Here are some of them.

1. In response to partner's double of a weak two-bid:

        (2♥)   Double   (Pass)   2NT: LEB.

2. In response to partner's reopening double of a two-level overcall:

        1♠   (2♥)   Pass   (Pass)
        Double (Pass)   2NT: LEB.

3. Partner makes a take-out double and they raise:

        (1♠)   Double   (2♠)   2NT: LEB.

The assumption is that LEB shows in these cases a weaker hand than bidding directly. It only makes sense in these auctions that direct three-level bids are INV and natural, which differs from the interpretation when partner opens 1NT.

        (2♥)   Double   (Pass)   3♣, 3♦

3♣, 3♦: values but non-forcing. I suggest a range of 9-11 HCP (maybe less with a long suit).

Some other aspects of '1NT opening LEB' don't correlate well to these other LEB sequences:

        (2♥)   Double   (Pass)   3NT

3NT: this just sounds like a desire to play 3NT, not 'slow with stopper'.

However, it is possible to assign meanings to a slow 3NT, or fast or slow cuebids. One possibility:

(2♥)   Double   (Pass)

3♥: no stopper, no four spades
3NT: to play

(2♥)   Double   (Pass)   2NT: LEB
(Pass)   3♣   (Pass)

3♥: four spades, no stopper
3NT: four spades, has stopper

The other auctions listed are less common and don't need a lot of details.

(1♠)   Double   (2♠)

2NT: LEB, weak hand competing to three-level
3♣, 3♦ or 3♥: values, game interest but non-forcing

1♠   (2♥)   Pass   (Pass)
Double   (Pass)

2NT: LEB, bad hand
3♣ or 3♦: values, non-forcing

There are a lot of things in this chapter for you to consider. I hope this helps you and your partner understand Lebensohl and how you might choose to use it.

8
Ogust

Introduction: Ogust 2NT asking and responses

Ogust was likely developed by the American player, deceased, Harold Ogust. In any event it bears his name and is a worthwhile convention to discover the quality of partner's hand when a weak two bid is opened.

When weak twos were first created a 2NT response was used to discover a side 'feature', normally defined as a side ace or king.

2♠   2NT

3♣: has a feature in clubs
3♦: has a feature in diamonds
3♥: has a feature in hearts
3♠: has no side-suit feature

That could work well on this type of deal:

♠ A Q 10 5 4 3	♠ K 9 2
♥ 3 2	♥ K Q 4
♦ K 3	♦ A Q 10 8 7
♣ 9 7 6	♣ A 8

2♠	2NT
3♦	4NT
5♦	6♠

3♦ shows a diamond feature, known to be the king given responder's holding. Responder then bids Roman Keycard Blackwood (RKC) into the slam. (Responder might choose to bid 5♥ to check for the trump queen if he plans to stop in 5♠ if opener lacks the ♠Q.) If opener had bid 3♠ to deny a feature responder would probably give up on slam.

In prior times weak twos generally were pretty 'sound'. If there was no side suit feature responder could count on opener having a pretty good suit. In more modern times, weak twos have gotten pretty weak, and the suit quality has been more variable. Using Ogust, the 2NT response asks for hand quality and suit quality rather than a specific feature.

2♠   2NT

3♣: 'bad bad' – bad hand, bad suit
3♦: 'bad hand, good suit'
3♥: 'good hand, bad suit'
3♠: 'good good' – good hand, good suit

What is a good suit? The way most people play it is a suit with at least 2 of the top 3 honors in the suit. KQ5432 would be a good suit, AJ10987 would be a bad suit. This might not strike you as sensible, but the reason would seem to be that responder wants to know that if he has the third top honor, that the suit should run, either for 3NT or for slam.

If instead you are interested in whether the suit is playable opposite shortness, you might wish to use different parameters, where an 'empty' suit (even with 2 of 3 tops) is not a good suit and a suit with strong intermediates (AJ109xx) is a good suit. It is up to you but I will stick with the standard interpretation where 2 of the 3 tops are required to show a good suit.

This deal shows the value of Ogust:

♠ K Q 7 6 4 3	♠ A 8
♥ J 8	♥ K 10 4 3
♦ 8 6 5	♦ A Q 3
♣ 10 3	♣ K 9 6 4

2♠	2NT
3♦	3NT

2NT is Ogust, and the 3♦ reply shows a bad hand but a good suit, KQxxxx or better given that responder has the ♠A. Bidding any game is aggressive, but 3NT has better play than 4♠ does. With a third spade and one less heart 3NT would be an even better bid.

The second question is "what is a good hand"? That depends first of all on your range for the weak two. If it is a 'sound' range, say 6-11, then 6-8 would be bad and 9-11 would be good. If a 'weaker range', say 5-10, then everything would move down 1 point.

I do think however that playing strength needs to be considered since responder is trying to decide whether or not to bid game (or less commonly, whether or not to bid slam). If he already knew the answer he would have blasted to game or bid RKC.

Playing strength starts with your HCP. Next look at your shape and honor location to make a modified judgment. Then consider how your hand fits in the range that your partnership has agreed for a weak two-bid.

Suppose your range is 5-11 for a weak two. What response would you give, using Ogust responses, to partner's 2NT reply?

1.   ♠ K 3
            ♥ Q 10 9 6 5 4
            ♦ 9 7 6
            ♣ J 3

2.   ♠ A J 10 7 6 5
            ♥ –
            ♦ Q 10 9 7
            ♣ 9 5 4

3.   ♠ A J 10 7 6 5
            ♥ Q 3
            ♦ 8 5 4
            ♣ 8 6

- Hand 1 has 6 HCP and nothing to recommend upgrading. The suit is bad and the hand is bad, respond 3♣.
- Hand 2 has 7 HCP but has excellent playing strength, including the void and the strong 4-card side suit. Bid 3♥ to show a good hand with a bad suit.
- Hand 3 has 7 HCP with identical spades and HCP as hand 2 but is a much weaker playing hand. Bid 3♣ to show 'bad bad'.

You might object to opening a weak two with one or more of the above hands. Hand 1 because the hand is too weak, and I would agree for sure if vulnerable vs. not. Nonvul I would open 2♥ and consider it a matter of judgment both vul. Hand 2 has a void which is a no-no to some players but not to me, as long as the void doesn't make the hand too strong for a weak two.

Ogust after a weak 2♦ opening

Of course you can keep the same responses as used over a major suit weak two. However, we might wish to stop in 3♦ when opener has a 3♥ 'good hand bad suit' reply which of course is not possible without changing the responses. I suggest this, then (all suggestions are subject to partnership understanding and approval):

2♦   2NT

3♣: either a medium or a maximum weak two
3♦: minimum weak two

Over 3♣, responder can bid 3♦ which is non-forcing but asks opener to bid again with a maximum weak two (especially one suited to 3NT since 5♦ is a less likely target contract).

♠ K 3	♠ A 7 6
♥ 9 3	♥ A J 8 2
♦ A Q 10 9 4 3	♦ J 2
♣ 10 7 6	♣ A 5 4 3

2♦	2NT
3♣	3♦
3NT	

3♣ shows a medium or maximum weak two. 3♦ is non-forcing, but still invitational. With a maximum that is suited to 3NT, opener bids 3NT.

What about rebids past 3♦? I think these are necessary only if a weak 2♦ opening is permissible with a 4-card major. Holding such a hand, and at least a medium quality hand, opener bids his 4-card major:

2♦   2NT

3♥: at least a medium weak two

with 4 hearts

The 3♥ bid is not game forcing – if responder returns to 4♦ opener is encouraged to pass.

♠ Q 9 6 5	♠ A K 10 4
♥ 2	♥ Q 8 3
♦ A Q J 7 6 5	♦ K 2
♣ 9 4	♣ K 8 6 5

2♦	2NT
3♠	4♠

3♠ shows at least a medium preempt with 4 spades and the vastly superior 4♠ is reached. Of course if you never open a weak 2♦ with a 4-card major you won't need this sequence.

Another advantage of the modified responses to Ogust are to allow responder to bid a Major suit at the 3-level, showing a forcing hand with at least a 5-card suit.

2♦	2NT
3♣	3♥: forcing one round,
	5+ hearts

♠ 2	♠ K 10 3
♥ J 9 8	♥ A Q 10 7 6
♦ A J 8 7 6 5	♦ K 3
♣ J 7 6	♣ A 10 2

2♦	2NT
3♦	3♥
4♥	

Those who like 'new suit forcing' over weak twos would respond 2♥, not 2NT. I prefer new suits non-forcing over weak twos, so I like to have room available to first bid 2NT then show my suit, forcing.

A 3NT reply to Ogust

Many pairs like to use a 3NT reply to Ogust to show a solid suit (AKQxxx, which of course might not actually run). This is useful information so I recommend it.

♠ A K Q 5 4 2	♠ 7 6 3
♥ 8 6 5	♥ A K 3
♦ 10 3	♦ Q 7 6 5 4
♣ 9 6	♣ A Q

2♠	2NT
3NT	

Opposite AKQxxx of spades 3NT looks safest.

Responder's continuations after hearing opener's reply

In most cases responder signs off in 3 or 4 of opener's major, or 3NT. In other cases responder can bid RKC for the major. If responder bids a new suit, that is presumably natural and forcing:

2♠	2NT
3♣	3♥: natural and forcing

Of course if you prefer new suits forcing over weak twos, then 3♥ could mean something at least a little bit different. For example,

3♥ directly could show 6+ hearts and 3♥ 'delayed' (i.e. bidding 2NT first then 3♥) could show 5 hearts.

Or, you could decide that if you bid 2NT then a new suit that you are cuebidding for a possible slam in opener's major.

I definitely prefer new suits non-forcing over weak twos as you pick up many more of those hands. However I suggest that regardless of this issue that you use a delayed 4♣ bid to show slam interest in the major:

2♠	2NT
3♣	4♣: should be slam interest in spades

A slam try in spades is a lot more likely than a forcing hand with clubs. One way to play is to show a slam try in spades, artificially. Opener cuebids if he can, and can bid RKC if he likes his hand sufficiently:

♠ A Q 9 7 6 5	♠ K 10 3
♥ 9 8 7	♥ A K Q J 3
♦ 2	♦ J 8 7
♣ 8 7 5	♣ A 3

2♠	2NT
3♦	4♣
4♦	4NT
5♦	6♠

3♦ showed a bad hand with a good suit. 4♣ is an artificial slam try in spades. Opener's cuebid of 4♦ tells responder what he needs to know and in reality responder should just bid 6♠ over 4♦ since opener can't have the ♦A in addition to a good suit for the 3♦ response.

Some prefer to play that a 4♣ continuation is RKC in the major. I don't like this as much as '4♣ slam try' as the previous deal illustrates, but it would look like this:

2♥	2NT
3♥	4♣: RKC in hearts

Some even play different responses to 4♣ RKC, often called 'Preempt Keycard' or 'PKC':

2♠	2NT
3♥	4♣: PKC

4♦: no keycards
4♥: 1 keycard, no trump queen
4♠: 1 keycard + trump queen
4NT: 2 keycards, no trump queen
5♣: 2 keycards + trump queen

I have never particularly seen the merit of this either. If it is important to use 4♣ as RKC, then we don't want a 'three step' response (4♠) to show only 1 keycard.

I suggest if you want to use PKC, use it as a direct 4♣ response:

♠ Q J 10 7 6 5	♠ K 9 4 2
♥ K Q 3	♥ 2
♦ Q 9 3	♦ A 2
♣ 7	♣ A K Q 9 8 6

2♠	4♣
4♦	4♠

It is useful to stop in 4♠ as a diamond lead might hold you to 10 tricks. 4♣ is RKC (or PKC if you prefer) and allows an easy stop in game.

Responder's continuations
after a weak 2♦ opening

Most of the issues are the same. Again, I suggest a jump to 4♣ directly over 2♦ is RKC (or PKC if you prefer). 2NT then 4♣ would be an artificial slam try in diamonds. Otherwise new suits are natural and forcing. Bidding diamonds at the lowest level is non-forcing.

♠ K 3	♠ A 4 2
♥ J 10 3	♥ A 8 4
♦ A Q 8 7 6 5	♦ K J 3
♣ 9 3	♣ J 8 4 2

2♦	2NT
3♣	3♦
3NT	

3♣ shows a non-minimum and responder bids a non-forcing, but still invitational, 3♦. With a total maximum opener has an easy 3NT bid.

Over the non-forcing 3♦ bid, opener can continue with 3♥ or 3♠. He has already denied a 4-card suit, so this should show an unbalanced hand. One simple idea is to show shortness (a singleton in the bid suit). Or, it can show shortness in a hand that has more interest in playing 5♦ than 3NT:

♠ 2	♠ J 8 6
♥ K 2	♥ A J 9 3
♦ Q J 9 8 6 5	♦ K 10 4 2
♣ K J 9 8	♣ A 2

2♦	2NT
3♣	3♦
3♠	5♦

3♠ shows spade shortness and interest in a suit contact. Responder has an easy acceptance with little wasted in spades and a good trump fit. Note that if responder had A86 of spades and Q2 of clubs 5♦ would still be the best spot.

Using Ogust in competition

If 2NT is still available to responder, I suggest 2NT should still be Ogust. (For clarity, opponents' bids are shown in brackets.)

2♥   (Double)   2NT: Ogust

2♦   (2♠)   2NT: Ogust

Responses would be the same as without the intervening bid.

If RHO overcalls, responder can cuebid (at the 3-level only) to see if opener can bid 3NT. This is most likely after a weak 2♦ opening.

♠ K 3	♠ 10 8 7
♥ 9 7	♥ A K 5 4
♦ K J 8 7 5 4	♦ A Q 9
♣ 8 6 5	♣ A 9 3

2♦   (2♠)   3♠   (Pass)

3NT

The bidding could end in 4♦ if opener can't bid 3NT.

Using Ogust to cater to 5-card weak two bids

In recent years many have been opening weak two bids with a 5-card suit. There are many ideas of what this should look like but I would suggest a fairly good suit. Having some side shape (i.e. not 5332) is also recommended. And of course, being nonvulnerable!

A 5-card weak two can be shown by modifying the responses to 2NT. The emphasis goes away from showing a good vs bad suit, to just showing the value range of the hand. If you have any tendency to open a weak two with a 5-card suit I recommend this:

2♠   2NT

3♣: "I have a 5-card weak two bid"
3♦: 6+ card weak two, minimum
3♥: 6+ card weak two, medium
3♠: 6+ card weak two, maximum
3NT: AKQxxx preempt

Quiz

What would you rebid over 2NT, '5 card Ogust' with these hands?

1.   ♠ A Q J 8 7
                ♥ 2
                ♦ J 10 7 6
                ♣ J 7 6

2.   ♠ 2
                ♥ K 9 8 7 6 5
                ♦ J 7 6 5
                ♣ 10 3

3.   ♠ K J 8 6 5 4 3
       ♥ K 3 2
       ♦ 8
       ♣ 7 6

ANSWERS

1. Bid 3♣, showing a 5-card weak two. This does not clarify whether you are minimum or maximum, and is artificial. Having only 5 trump you would normally have a fairly good suit.
2. Bid 3♦, showing at least a 6-card suit and a minimum.
3. Bid 3♠, showing a maximum with 6+ trump.

Perhaps you would open a weak two with only some, or none, of these hands. 5-card weak twos like hand 1 are best nonvul. Bad hands like hand 2 are also best nonvul. Hand 3 would be a 3♠ opening but perhaps not when vul, or vul vs not.

Responder's continuation having bid 5-card Ogust

In most cases continuations would mean the same as they would have had 2NT been normal Ogust. The only exception is over the 3♣ "I have a 5-card weak two" response:

2♥	2NT
3♣	3♦: "tell me more"

3♥: minimum
3NT: maximum, no singleton
3♠: maximum, unbalanced (has a side singleton)

The responses are actually to rebid 3 of the opened major to show a minimum, 3 of the other major to show an unbalanced maximum. This is most logical to me and allows a stop in 3 of the major when opener has a minimum. You might prefer to use step responses (3♥ = minimum, 3♠ = maximum unbalanced, 3NT = maximum balanced) but I will assume my suggested responses above. How might this pair of hands be bid?

♠ A Q J 8 7	♠ K 9 3
♥ 2	♥ A K 8 6 5
♦ Q J 8 7	♦ K 2
♣ 9 7 6	♣ A K 3

I suggest this possible auction:

2♠	2NT
3♣	3♦
3♥	4♣
4NT	5♣
6♠	

3♣ showed a 5-card weak two and 3♦ asked for more information. 3♥, the other major, showed a maximum and unbalanced. 4♣, bid after 2NT, shows a slam try in opener's suit. With a very good hand opener takes over with RKC.

An alternate meaning for a 3NT rebid over 2NT

Perhaps showing AKQxxx is not so worthwhile, either because you would open a 1-bid with that, or because just showing a maximum is sufficient. That would free up a 3NT rebid. What should it show?

I think it should show a reasonable preempt with 4 of the other major. Assuming this is the case, how would the hands below be bid?

♠ J 10 8 7	♠ K Q 9 4
♥ K Q 10 7 6 5	♥ 4
♦ K 3	♦ A Q 6 5 2
♣ 3	♣ A K 2
2♥	2NT
3NT	4♠

3NT shows 4 of the other major and a reasonable+ weak two. This allows the best game to be reached.

Final recommendations and conclusion

Ogust is a useful convention, though if your preempts are 'classic' showing a side feature could be just as good a method.

If you have any tendency to open weak twos with a 5-card suit I recommend 5-card Ogust. Perhaps you should play normal Ogust when vulnerable and 5-card Ogust when nonvulnerable.

Part of the fun is for each partnership to explore these ideas.

9
Exclusion Blackwood & Lackwood

Introduction

Blackwood, of course, is the convention to ask partner for the number of aces he holds. It is credited to Easley Blackwood, who I knew pretty well back in my Indiana days. Players learned that counting 'points' doesn't work so well on distributional hands, especially when you are considering a slam. Suppose you have the following hand, with partner showing a good raise of your 1♠ opening:

♠ K Q 10 8 7 6
♥ 2
♦ A K Q 8 7
♣ 4

Partner could have either of these opening hands with spade support:

	1.			2.	
	♠	A J 9 4		♠	A 9 4 3
	♥	K Q J 8		♥	A 8 7
	♦	J 3		♦	9 2
	♣	K Q 10		♣	A 8 6 5

Hand 1 has 17 HCP but the vast majority of those points are wasted. All you can make is game in spades.

Hand 2 has only 12 HCP but has just the values you need – 3 aces plus a good trump fit. 7♠ is almost laydown and should be bid.

Thus, Blackwood and the more advanced versions of Blackwood are attempts to answer this question: "does partner have the RIGHT values to fit my hand?". Of course, Blackwood can't answer that question when your hand has good controls, especially aces, but lacks secondary values. Suppose opener's hand was instead this:

♠ A 10 8 7 6 5
♥ A
♦ A 8 7 6 5
♣ A

Opener has all the aces so asking for partner's aces is obviously fruitless. Slam is still possible but partner needs the right values, in your long suits, such as one of these hands:

	3.			4.	
	♠	K 9 4 3		♠	K J 4 3
	♥	9 7 6		♥	K 7 6 5
	♦	Q J 3		♦	K 2
	♣	K Q 3		♣	J 3 2

Both hands above would be limit raises of a 1♠ opening. Hand 3 has a good enough diamond holding to hold your losses to one trick, and spades are probably 2-1 solidifying trump.

Hand 4 has a 'magic' holding in your second suit, diamonds, and 7♠ is a good (but not cold) contract. Both of these hands have some wasted values yet slam is good so bidding Blackwood wouldn't be the worst thing. It would be better to show a second suit of diamonds then get into some scientific bidding.

How to do the above is beyond the scope of this book, but the point is that some hands are suited for Blackwood and some are not.

Back when I had been playing only a couple of years, Keycard Blackwood was developed. The king of trumps has great value such that it could be considered like an ace. Thus there were now 5 'aces', or 'keycards'. At least if you bid Blackwood on the previous hand, you would discover that partner has the missing keycard, the ♠K. You could then continue to ask and if you play 'specific kings', then you might discover the ♦K but not that partner has the magic holding of doubleton ♦K.

Not long after Keycard Blackwood came Roman Keycard Blackwood, where the queen of trump is shown. The queen of trump is important but does not rise to the level of a keycard. When you have a 10+ card trump fit, as in the examples above, the trumps figure to split 2-1 which removes the need to own the trump queen. Of course trump might split 3-0 and so the queen isn't worthless but you don't want to consider it to be as valuable as the trump king.

Since we will be discussing Exclusion Roman Keycard Blackwood, another version, let's review the responses to Roman Keycard Blackwood (hereafter called 'RKC'):

OPENER	RESPONDER	
1♠	3♠	
4NT	5♣:	0 or 3 keycards
	5♦:	1 or 4 keycards
	5♥:	2 keycards, no trump queen
	5♠:	2 keycards, has trump queen

These are the 'standard' responses. Many prefer to reverse the meaning of the 5♣ and 5♦ responses, so step 1 (5♣) shows 1 or 4 keycards, while 5♦ shows 0 or 3. 1-4-3-0, thus the name '1430'. I won't debate the merits of 1430 here, but of course you must know which version your partnership uses.

If the trump queen has not been shown nor denied (a 5♣ or 5♦ response), then the cheapest bid that is NOT the trump suit (which would be a sign-off), asks for the trump queen. The standard responses are:

- returning to trump at the cheapest level = denying the trump queen
- jumping to slam in the trump suit = has the trump queen, but no side suit Kings (the king of trump is shown as a keycard)
- bidding another suit = showing the king of the bid suit, and the queen of trump in addition; if two kings are held, cuebid the cheaper

This deal shows RKC in action:

OPENER	RESPONDER
♠ A Q 7 6	♠ K 9 8 3 2
♥ A 8 7	♥ 2
♦ K 2	♦ A Q 9 8 3
♣ A 8 7 6	♣ K 3
1NT	2♥
3♠	4NT
5♣	5♦
6♦	7♠

After the Jacoby transfer, opener jumps to 3♠ to show a good hand with at least 4 trump. Over 4NT (RKC), opener bids the first step, 5♣, to show 0 or 3 keycards. Responder knows from the bidding it is "3". He bids the cheapest available bid, 5♦, to ask for the queen of trump. Opener's 6♦ bid shows the trump queen + the ♦K, but denies the 'cheaper' kings in hearts or clubs.

Exclusion RKC

This was a quick review of RKC; for more details read the topic on the subject (in Eric Rodwell's bidding topics book 1). Exclusion RKC is used when 'asker' (the player using RKC) has a void. He wants partner to show keycards but to EXCLUDE the ace of the void suit. Change the hands to this:

OPENER	RESPONDER
♠ A Q 7 6	♠ K 9 8 4 3 2
♥ A Q 8	♥ K 2
♦ K 10 3	♦ A Q 9 7 6
♣ Q 8 3	♣ —
1NT	2♥
3♠	5♣
?	

Note that there are some questions we have to answer first.

How do we employ Exclusion RKC? It is normally played by making an 'impossible' jump to the 5-level. On the above deal, spades have been firmly agreed so the 5♣ jump cannot be to play in a 5♣ contract. Those who play Exclusion RKC play such impossible jumps as 'Exclusion' as it is called.

How do we respond to Exclusion? I recommend the same step response structure that you use when playing RKC – the first step shows 0 or 3 keycards, the second step shows 1 or 4 keycards, etc. Switch steps 1 and 2 if you play '1430' responses. I won't say this again; make the adjustments in later examples.

Thus the auction from the example above would go:

OPENER	RESPONDER
1NT	2♥
3♠	5♣
5NT	

For those not so familiar with Exclusion, it might be tough to work out what the response shows. You are used to replies to 4NT – 5♣ is the first step, 5♦ the second step, etc. When RKC is a bid in a suit, you have to abandon this thinking and count the steps: 5♦ = 0 or 3, 5♥ = 1 or 4, 5♠ = 2 with no trump queen, so 5NT shows 2 + the trump queen.

At this point responder needs to take stock. There are only FOUR Keycards, with the ♣A thrown out – excluded. Opener has shown two and responder has two which means that no important keycards are missing.

There is a 6-4 trump fit so that suit is solid. Responder has ♥Kx opposite the ace. The only question is "how do I find out if opener has the ♦K?".

You may have noticed that there isn't much space available. Thus, I suggest that bidding 6 of a suit says "bid a grand slam if you have the king of this suit".

The complete auction would be:

OPENER	RESPONDER
1NT	2♥
3♠	5♣
5NT	6♦
7♠	

Well done! However, switch the heart and club suits and the bidding is much more cramped:

OPENER	RESPONDER
1NT	2♥
3♠	5♥
6♦	?

Now there is no room to ask about the ♦K.

There are some high-tech ideas that come to mind, but for now, responder might control-bid 4♣, hoping to hear opener bid 4♦. I do recommend, that when a major is agreed and partner has expressed slam potential, that second round controls can be cuebid.

The bidding would then be:

OPENER	RESPONDER
1NT	2♥
3♠	4♣
4♦	5♥
6♦	7♠

How can responder figure out to bid this way? By anticipating what would happen in the various auctions that might arise. Think to yourself "if I jump to 5♥ and opener bids 6♦, I won't have room to ask for the ♦K. So, I need to try to get him to cuebid the ♦K first".

Of course, the devil fools with the best made plan. What if opener doesn't bid 4♦, but bids 4♥ or 4♠? This is a matter of part-nership style, but I have said in previous topics, that "what you bypass, you deny". Thus, not bidding 4♦ over 4♣ would deny the ♦K.

This means that you are unlikely to want to be in a grand slam (opener would need a good source of tricks to pitch all the dia-mond losers from your hand, and you have no way to find that out).

Thus, you might just jump to 6♠. Looking at the hand again:

♠ K 9 8 4 3 2
♥ —
♦ A Q 9 7 6
♣ K 2

You could ask yourself "might we wish to stop in game"? Clearly if you are missing two aces you would. You have 12 HCP and opener shows 16 or 17. 16+12=28. You are missing the ♦K so it is just possible but quite unlikely that opener is missing also two aces.

One thing you could do, over 4♥, is bid 4NT. If two aces are missing, figure that partner probably has the ♥A and sign off in 5♠. After all, even if only one ace is missing you might not make six due to the ♦K missing.

You could also bid 5♥, if playing normal and not 1430 responses, since if opener bids 5♠ he is missing both useful aces, and if he bids 5NT (one working ace) at least slam should have play. This works only if 5♥ as a NON-jump is used as Exclusion (not a common treatment).

In summary, Exclusion is not a cure-all. It involves jumping to a high level and the responses may either get you too high, or preclude further investigation for a grand slam.

Is it Exclusion, or natural?

As usual, this is a matter for your own discussion with partner. I say, if no suit is agreed, a 5-level jump is Exclusion only if the player making that bid has denied a long suit there, or if it is truly impossible as a natural bid.

Examples:

OPENER	RESPONDER
1♠	5♣

OPENER	RESPONDER
1♥	1♠
5♣	

In the first case, responder is showing something like KQJxxxxxx in clubs and out so 5♣ should be natural. In the second auction, there is no need with hearts and clubs to jump to 5♣ – opener can force by bidding 3♣. Thus, 5♣ should be Exclusion RKC, agreeing spades, the last natural suit.

Responder could have a weak hand with weak spades, so opener needs a very good hand to use Exclusion at this point. This hand would qualify:

♠ K Q 10 8 7
♥ A K 9 8 7 6
♦ K Q
♣ –

Even with this hand it is not 100% – responder might have xxxx in spades or xxx in hearts, but it is about as good as you are going to get without a hand that should have opened 2♣.

What about competitive auctions? It is easy to recognize a 5-level jump in the opponent's suit as Exclusion (L/RHO stands for Left/Right Hand Opponent):

OPENER	LHO	RESPONDER	RHO
1♥	Pass	2♦	3♣
5♣			

This is clearly Exclusion RKC for diamonds. What about jumps to the 5-level in new suits? To me it matters if a lower bid in that suit would have been forcing:

OPENER	LHO	RESPONDER	RHO
1♦	Pass	1♠	3♥
5♣			

Only my team coach Eric Kokish would suggest that a 4♣ bid here should be forcing. Thus, jumping to 5♣ should be natural. Opener might have a hand like this:

♠ 2
♥ —
♦ K Q J 8 7 6
♣ A K 10 7 6 5

Compare with this sequence:

OPENER	LHO	RESPONDER	RHO
1♠	Pass	2♦	3♥
5♣			

Since 2♦ is game forcing (please, tell me you play it game forcing!), there is no reason not to bid 4♣, forcing, with clubs.

Thus, 5♣ should be Exclusion RKC. Even if two-over-one is not game forcing, opener's new suit (4♣) at the 4-level would be forcing.

Getting into Exclusion at a lower level

One trick is to have this rule: when you make a splinter bid, then bid RKC, this is Exclusion.

OPENER	RESPONDER
1♠	4♥
4♠	4NT: Exclusion with a heart void

This assumes that you play the jump to 4♥ as a splinter, not as natural. Another thing to discuss! Let's see how saving space versus having to bid 5♥ can work to advantage:

OPENER	RESPONDER
♠ A J 8 7 6	♠ K 10 4 3 2
♥ A Q 3	♥ —
♦ 10 3 2	♦ K Q J 8 7
♣ 3 2	♣ K Q 10

1♠	4♥
4♠	4NT
5♦	5♠

It isn't great to be in 5♠, but if responder had to bid 5♥ the 5NT response would result in slam off two aces.

Another idea: playing splinters show a void, or certain splinter sequences as showing voids, such as this:

OPENER	RESPONDER
1♠	3NT: singleton splinter in any suit
4♣: where?	4♦: ♦-singleton
	4♥: ♥-singleton
	4♠: ♣-singleton

Or, your 'coding' might be by steps, where 4♦ = ♣-singleton, 4♥ = ♦-singleton, and 4♠ = ♥-singleton.

This means that direct splinters can show voids:

OPENER	RESPONDER
1♠	4♣, 4♦, or 4♥: void-showing splinters

It is better to stop in 4♠ and not use Exclusion RKC at all if we are missing two important keycards (and perhaps other assets).

OPENER	RESPONDER
♠ Q 8 7 6 5	♠ K J 9 4 3
♥ A Q 8	♥ —
♦ K 3	♦ Q J 10 8 7
♣ Q 8 7	♣ A 10 3

1♠	4♥
4♠	

If 4♥ shows a void, responder can comfortably pass opener's return to 4♠.

There can be other sequences where a void can be shown economically:

Showing a singleton, then cuebidding the suit later shows a void (not singleton ace):

OPENER	RESPONDER
1♥	2NT
3♣	3♠
4♣	

If 2NT is a forcing heart raise ('Jacoby 2NT') and 3♣ shows shortness in clubs, opener's later 4♣ bid then confirms a void.

In a two-over-one auction, when the major is agreed at the 2-level, opener shows his pattern with non-jump bids. Thus, jumps can show voids:

OPENER	RESPONDER	
1♠	2♣	
2♥	2♠:	3-card forcing spade raise

3♣: clubs also, so singleton in diamonds, the fourth suit
4♣: VOID in clubs

Summary on Exclusion RKC

It is a useful convention but one with plenty of pitfalls. Be sure to do some work with your partner to practice and clarify things. As I said it is useful to have lower-level ways to show voids so that you can judge whether to move toward slam at all, and to have room to get information if you do later use any form of RKC.

Lackwood

Lackwood is a convention I devised about 30 years ago. 'Lack' means you are saying you lack control in a specific suit, and that partner needs a control in that suit to bid a slam. 'Wood' of course refers to Blackwood—if partner has first round control of the 'lack suit', then a grand slam is possible and he should give RKC responses:

OPENER	LHO	RESPONDER
1♠	4♥	5♠: 'Lackwood'

Responder has a big hand but has two fast heart losers. He wants opener to pass if he also has two heart losers. With second-round control, opener bids 6♠. With first round control, opener SHOWS keycards, starting with the first step – 5NT in this auction.

OPENER 1	RESPONDER
♠ Q J 10 7 6	♠ A K 9 5 4
♥ Q 3	♥ 10 2
♦ K Q J 8 7	♦ A
♣ Q	♣ A K J 7 6

OPENER 2
♠ Q J 10 7 6
♥ Q
♦ K Q J 8 7
♣ Q 2

OPENER 3
- ♠ Q J 10 7 6
- ♥ A 3
- ♦ K Q 8 7 3
- ♣ 2

OPENER 1	LHO	RESPONDER	RHO
1♠	4♥	5♠	Pass
Pass			

OPENER 2	LHO	RESPONDER	RHO
1♠	4♥	5♠	Pass
6♠			

In example 1, the jump to 5 of our major, when obviously we could have tried to play it at the 4-level, is 'Lackwood'. This shows a huge fitting hand but with two fast losers in their suit, hearts. Opener also has two heart losers so he passes.

In example 2, opener has a stiff heart, second round control. This he shows by bidding slam, 6♠. There is no thought of a grand slam because they can cash the ♥A.

Lackwood in action on example 3:

OPENER 3	LHO	RESPONDER	RHO
1♠	4♥	5♠	Pass
6♣	Pass	7♠	

Opener's response, 6♣, shows first round heart control and 1 or 4 keycards. This is all responder needs to know and he bids the grand slam. He is willing to gamble a bit on the club suit, hoping opener has the ♣Q, two or fewer clubs, or a lucky location of the ♣Q. Opener might also have a good enough diamond suit to discard three clubs from dummy.

Showing a void in their suit as a keycard

Since a Lackwood jump to 5 of the major denies the ace of their suit, opener can show a void as a keycard! Give opener this hand:

♠ Q J 10 6 2
♥ —
♦ K Q J 7 6
♣ Q 9 4

and he would bid 6♣ to show one keycard – the heart void – and responder could bid 7♠.

Lackwood in a constructive auction

It must be clear what suit is lacking in a control or partner will have no idea whether or not to accept the invitation. Sometimes there is one suit that might be uncontrolled from the prior bidding:

Opener	Responder
1♠	2♥
3♥	4♦
4♥	?

Responder might have a big hand like:

♠ A
♥ A Q J 9 6 5
♦ A K J 4
♣ 8 3

Opener might have control in clubs but not enough values to have bid past game to show that club control over your 4♦ bid. Opener might for example have this hand:

♠ K J 8 7 5
♥ K 10 3
♦ 8 6
♣ A 10 5

A raise to 5♥ is Lackwood, asking for control in clubs, the only suit that wasn't either bid naturally nor cuebid earlier. In this case, opener has first round club control so he would bid 6♣, the third step, to show two keycards + first round control of clubs.

Now responder has to guess whether to bid 7 or not, but he can bid 6♦, the only available bid, as a sort of 'Last Train' asking if opener can bid 7. It is not clear that he would; the doubleton diamond and ♥10 turn out to be key values. But, give him instead ♠ K Q 8 7 5 and he should bid 7♥ over your 6♦ Last Train bid.

The full auction:

OPENER	RESPONDER
1♠	2♥
3♥	4♦
4♥	5♥
6♣	6♦
7♥	

Using a 5NT response to show the guarded king of the lack suit

There can be an advantage in playing in 6NT, played from the hand with Kx(x) in the suit, instead of slam in the agreed suit, for two reasons:

1. it prevents them leading ace and another to give partner a ruff, or
2. if the hand with xx would be declarer, it avoids a trick one lead through the Kx in dummy.

If you want to make this addition, you could do it this way:

OPENER	LHO	RESPONDER	RHO
1♠	4♥	5♠	Pass

5NT: Kx(x) in hearts
6♣: EVEN number of keycards, first round control of hearts
6♦: ODD number of keycards, first round control of hearts

Go back to the 1♠-4♥ examples earlier, and you will see that with Kx of hearts it is surely better to try 6NT than risk the player who leapt to 4♥ leading ace and giving partner a heart ruff.

Conclusion

Lackwood is a useful convention but it comes up rarely. One reason is that a hand with two fast losers in a key suit doesn't very often have everything so well covered that they can be sure that, even if partner has the missing control, that there aren't two keycards missing. Just the same, it is another tool to have in your kit just in case you need it.

Good luck!